THE
COMPLETE
PROFESSIONAL
SALESMAN

*the text of this book is printed
on 100% recycled paper*

The Complete Professional Salesman

by
ROBERT L. SHOOK *and* **HERBERT M. SHOOK**

Written with the Assistance of:
Ron Bingaman, Vice President -
Public Relations,
Management Horizons, Inc.
Columbus, Ohio

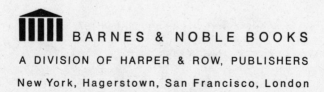

BARNES & NOBLE BOOKS
A DIVISION OF HARPER & ROW, PUBLISHERS
New York, Hagerstown, San Francisco, London

This book is dedicated
to the Free Enterprise System
and the Salesmen of the world
who perpetuate it.

A hardcover edition of this book is published by Frederick Fell, Inc.,
under the title *How to Be the Complete Professional Salesman*. It is here
reprinted by arrangement.

First BARNES & NOBLE BOOKS edition published 1975

STANDARD BOOK NUMBER: 06–463433–7

76 77 78 79 80   12 11 10 9 8 7 6 5 4 3 2

CONTENTS

PREFACE

The Complete Professional Salesman offers a new concept in selling. It combines effective selling techniques and self-confidence-builders to produce a new dimension in selling . . . "sales-confidence." This book mixes these two important ingredients into a dynamic one-two punch aimed at helping you add to your professionalism as a salesman.

The book will not benefit the run-of-the-mill salesman. *The Complete Professional Salesman* is geared to the needs of the *elite* in our society of professional salesmen. It has been written for the man who takes his work to heart—for the dedicated man who aims for the *very top* in his field. It treats a career in selling not as a job, but as a *profession*. It recognizes that the professional salesman thrives on being an expert in every facet of his work.

All of us are approached by hundreds of salespeople every year; but few of us can think of more than a handful of salesmen we consider to be *professional*.

Every salesman has the opportunity to become a professional. Yet, only a small percentage will fit into this select group. It won't be by accident that *you* will become a member. You'll have to work hard. You'll have to develop a certain "magic" quality which you will find to be a common denominator shared by all top salesmen. Sales-confidence is that *winning* quality which you must develop if you want to reach the pinnacle of success in the selling field.

You must approach a career in selling like a professional does in any other field. You can't just assume that you'll become a professional salesman by making many years of "calls" on your prospects. You must realize that without a planned and systematic approach to selling, you'll never achieve the finesse (or perhaps even the basic fundamentals) which the *masters* in the sales field possess. Consider the fact that there are millions of golfers in the United States—and yet, how many of them are *pros?* If you have ever played golf, you will know that no matter how many times you swing at the ball, you'll never shoot in the low seventies unless you learn how to swing the club correctly. It certainly doesn't come naturally. It's something that has to be learned—and then *practiced.* Everybody tries to make other people laugh. Everybody wants to be a comedian. Yet perhaps only a few dozen individuals out of two hundred million in the United States actually make a living at it! Obviously, these are two extreme examples in two unrelated professions. But they *do* relate to the elusive quality of *success.* Although the odds aren't quite as greatly stacked against you in the sales field, perhaps you should nonetheless take the attitude that they *are.* Perhaps you should make yourself as devoted as, say, Jack Nicklaus, Arnold Palmer, Dick Van Dyke or Flip Wilson are in their fields. If you take this attitude, the odds will actually be *with* you! (See chapter XIX on *Practice, Practice, Practice, and Then Practice Some More,* and you will note that a professional salesman has a lot in common with professional athletes and entertainers!)

The Complete Professional Salesman is designed to make you a professional salesman in every facet of selling. You will learn *why* people buy. It's not enough to go out to "sell" a prospect—you must also know what it is that *motivates him to buy!*

Several chapters in the book are designed to help you develop *the selling pattern*—how to effectively approach a prospect or a buyer—how to give an effective presentation. And, naturally, how to *close* the sale!

While following the selling patterns and the many interesting techniques used to fully develop them, you will learn how to use *Control Selling* as a means of getting your prospect's full, undivided attention. You will learn how to use showmanship—a quality which really makes your work more exciting and fun!

Although the average salesman is continually worried about his prospect giving objections, you will soon be looking forward to them as *challenges*. You'll be wanting to meet these challenges head-on. For those salesmen who want to really create some additional "need" there's a chapter on *Reverse Selling*. You haven't seen anything until you've seen reverse selling in action! Yet these techniques of effective selling will not work unless you know how to develop the proper working habits and unless you know how to get the exposure necessary to use them. Learn how to put a value on your time. Find out how to set up your territory, so that you can make the most of every day.

After you have read *The Complete Professional Salesman,* we suggest that you read it again—and then again! You must not only read it, but you must also begin to *live* it.

The Complete Professional Salesman will add a new dimension to your life. You will enjoy your work and look forward to each day's selling with enthusiasm and zeal. You will also make more money with seemingly less effort than ever before.

Does all this sound too good to be true? Perhaps it is. But, once you have acquired that magic quality of sales-confidence, you'll discover a lot of new doors open to you . . . doors to a *new life!*

INTRODUCTION

A career in sales can cover a lot of ground. It can range from the service station attendant to the grocery clerk or the soda jerk at the drug store, to the highly astute businessman who sells million-dollar deals. Without question, no other profession in the world consists of such a diversification in terms of product, education, background and INCOME. There are people who call themselves salesmen whose earnings border the poverty-income levels, and there are those who generate annual incomes in excess of a *million dollars!*

There are some who literally make hundreds of times more income than others selling identical products . . . and, in many cases, even for the same company! If you don't believe this to be a fact, check with any large life insurance company whose licensed agents have identical policies to sell, and you'll discover that the top producers are earning more than a hundred times what the lowest producers are making. A quick review of real estate salesmen in any major city will reveal a similar situation. One may ask, *How is this possible? What is it that the leading salesmen do that projects such a vast difference in their performance?*

A quick analysis will reveal many surprises. A person who is unfamiliar with the sales world will discover that the big producers, as a group, do not necessarily possess the benefits which a higher education would permit. Nor do they possess the charm and sophistication that only a social-registered, prep school gentleman would be expected to have. Contrary to public opinion, a review of the top producers in this country would show that a high percentage of these leading salesmen were the product of poor immigrant families who did not have the means of having them college-educated.

There is also an American myth that says success in the sales field comes only as a result of a "dynamic sales personality." Again, a quick review of a large group of leading salesmen from different fields would reveal that they do not possess the stereotyped sales personalities which would be expected of them. Sure, a few of these top producers will have a dynamic sales personality, but that quality in itself would not be an important factor in their success (it can be assumed that a survey made among any group of individuals in any particular occupation will reveal the same percentage of "dynamic sales personalities"). What *is* it, then, that causes such a tremendous difference in the fluctuation of salesmen's productivity? What is the secret which a successful salesman can possess that literally earns him an income equivalent to that of a hundred of his cohorts?

It is the belief of the authors of this book that the combination of *mental attitude, work habits* and *professional salesmanship* are the three necessary qualities which most accurately describe the *highly successful salesman.* Although each of these qualities is of equal importance, this book will not dwell on mental attitude in detail *(see Chapter 3)* since this subject can consist of a complete volume of books by itself. Nor will we discuss in detail proper work habits, since the subject of *self-discipline* is also a complex topic in itself. Instead, the contents of this book will be confined to the discussion of *proven successful selling techniques* which are part-and-parcel with *professional salesmanship.*

The philosophy of this book is to approach salesmanship as a *career.* The field of selling requires the same professional attitude as do our sciences. Likewise, the "student of salesmanship" should not accept the ordinary hit-and-miss techniques which are so commonly employed by the vast armies of salesmen throughout the United States. Instead, our school of thought demands a more scientific approach which will fully develop any individual who has the desire to be successful.

It is suggested that you read this book in its entirety, and then on a weekly basis; read each Chapter on a Sunday night and consciously apply its lesson to your sales career Monday through Friday. The mere reading of the contents of this book will not by itself make you a professional salesman. It is suggested that you read it, digest it, practice it, and then execute it. After you have done this for a period of time you will be on your way to becoming a *professional salesman.*

I

SO YOU WANT TO BE
A SALESMAN

Wonderful! If your desire is sincere, if you have enough ambition, and if you have self-discipline—*then* you can become a successful salesman.

But remember: Success is a demanding mistress. She is jealous! Her favors come only at a high price, and you must be willing to pay it! If you want success, it must be *earned.*

Salesmanship is one of the finest professions on earth, and since you have chosen it, you are to be congratulated for a wise choice. It's a choice that can lead you and your family to a lifetime of prosperity and security. And, having made this choice, you can never again claim that the opportunity for success did not present itself. The rewards for the professional salesman are practically limitless.

But all this doesn't mean that you will *automatically* prosper—that you can simply sit back and wait for the rewards. In sales, as in anything else that pays high dividends, *you have to invest something first.* This old lesson, of course, has been preached to us over and over again. When we were students, we were told this about our school work. Our coaches also drilled this message into us in their pep talks. Even our clergymen preach it. It applies to all walks of life. If you want something of value, you must *reach* for it.

There are certain ingredients that make a winner, no matter what field you're competing in. The two most basic ingredients (assuming that you already have the desire, ambition and self-discipline) are *hard work* and *knowledge.*

We all know the importance of hard work. Few of us have ever known a successful *lazy* man!

Thomas Edison claimed:	"Success is 95 percent perspiration and 5 percent inspiration."
Michelangelo said:	"If people knew how hard I work to get my mastery, it wouldn't seem so wonderful at all."
And from Alexander Hamilton:	"All the genius I may have is merely the fruit of labor and thought."

This book will not dwell on the subject of hard work, because hard work is a habit that only *you* can develop for yourself.

Assuming that you either have this habit or you're successfully developing it, we *can,* however, offer some help on the subject of *knowledge.*

You must realize that selling takes a great deal more than simply knowing the product, knowing the company, knowing the territory and understanding the terms. The science of selling must be mastered like all other professions. The golf pro, for example, must master the science of his game through lessons and practice. Likewise, a man doesn't become a doctor merely by wanting to be one and working hard at it. He must learn the *science* of medicine through years of studying at medical school and more years of practicing as an intern and resident. Obviously, you too must know both the science and the art of salesmanship if you are to become a professional salesman. You must learn how to apply certain scientific principles of selling, and you must practice to fine-tune the artistry in selling.

The entire purpose of this book is to help you develop scientific knowledge in the art of salesmanship and to teach you how to become a professional salesman.

The Salesman's Role in Society

Selling is a key part—an *indispensable* part—of a free enterprise system. You, as a salesman, occupy a special niche in this system. Without you and your fellow salesmen, our standard of living would be far different, and our system would probably collapse. To a very great extent, we owe our affluent way of life in the Western World to the salesmen, past and present, who move the goods and services from producers to users. Because of the salesman, the wheels of industry are kept turning; income is created; and our standard of living flourishes. So—you see—the salesman can have a very *important role* in our society and, as a salesman, you should feel tremendous pride in your work.

Basically, of course, almost *all* of us are salesmen in one sense of the word or another. Everybody is selling *something*—either himself and his talents, a product, a service, an idea or a way of life. The fact is that, no matter whether you live in a capitalist society, a communist society, or on some remote island in the South Seas, you are selling something every time you smile or open you mouth. This, of course, is *not* "professional" selling. And *professional* selling is the real subject of our book. A capitalist society such as ours has to have large numbers of *professional* salesmen. Our economy is so finely tuned that the role of the salesman has become progressively more important and more complex. In this era of mass production and scientific marketing, goods and services *must* be moved or we will have *overproduction*. Our entire economy, thus, is highly *dependent upon good salesmanship.*

Selling in the Future

The future for the salesman—which means *your* future—is filled with challenge and excitement and opportunity. There are new horizons in many industries and new sales needs opening up in many new and specialized fields. Consider just a few, for example:

electronics, aerospace, chemistry, computers, engineering, ocea-nography, air pollution, building trades, education, insurance, banking, medicine, and many more. All of these fields need energetic and imaginative salesmen. It will take more know-how, improved skills, and extra effort to be successful in these fields—but at the same time the stakes will be much greater, and earnings will be higher than ever before.

In our supersonic age—with planes breaking the sound barrier, and speed and mobility ever on the increase—the world is constantly "shrinking" in size. A new breed of salesman has to be groomed for this kind of environment. He will have to be more sophisticated than his older brother. He will have to be scientifically trained. He will have to know how to do business on a much *broader scope*—an *international* scope. He will not only sell goods and services, but he will also sell good will—and he will play an important role in politics. The salesman is about to enter a new era; he is about to see doors opened that were closed to him in the past.

Conclusion

Everyone must know where he wants to go, and everyone must think long and hard about what he has to do to get there. In other words, everyone needs a goal to shoot at—a "pot of gold" at the end of the rainbow. This provides the incentive, the challenge, the direction, the fuel to motivate us in our quest for success. Set your sights high, but be realistic. If you are sincere in your efforts, you will succeed. Fortunately, there are enough challenging opportunities in the sales field to satisfy the appetites of the most enterprising people. If you are sincere in your desire to be a success, then work intelligently and diligently toward your goal. The decision is yours to make.

II

THE CUSTOMER: YOUR BREAD AND BUTTER

As a professional salesman you must always remember that without the customer there would be no need for your product, your company or your job. Satisfying the customer's needs is what your company is in business for, and your foremost thought every moment of your working day should be: "What can I do for my customer?"

It almost goes without saying that you should always treat him with courtesy, respect and good will. But above all, you must be *completely honest* with him. If you believe that your product is *not* best suited to his interests or would *not* render him the service that he expects, then don't hesitate to tell him so. You are going to be in business for a long time—not just for a few one-shot sales. Don't burn your bridges behind you, because tomorrow they may be very important to you. When you think of your future, think also of your customer—because your future depends on him.

The Company's Image

The image of your company depends on the image that you as a sales representative create. No matter what the size of your company, your personal contacts with its customers and prospects create more lasting impressions than almost any other single factor. After all, a company is only an organization made up of *people*. The customer may never even meet another representative of your company; and his opinion of you—favorable or unfavorable—will greatly influence his attitude toward your company. It will help him answer some very important questions: *"Is this company sincere?" "What kind of service will I get?" "Are they only interested in my dollars—not my needs?" "Are they progressive?" "Is this company going to stand behind its product?"* You, as the ambassador of your company, will most likely determine most of his answers.

Stop and think for a moment of a person you might have met from a foreign country—a country which you know very little about. After talking to this person, your opinion of his country will be greatly influenced by your conversation with him. For example, you will tend to regard his political opinions as those of his countrymen or possibly his country's government. More than likely you will also tend to generalize about his religious philosophy. If you get to know him well, you will soon find yourself speaking as an authority about his country. We all tend to do this sort of thing unconsciously.

Remember, too, that the same thing is probably happening with the other fellow. He is likewise generalizing about America and Americans from his impressions of you.

In the same manner, you as a salesman are continously the image of your company in the eyes of your customers.

The "Personal Touch" with the Customer

Naturally, certain friendships are going to exist between you as a salesman and most of your customers. Cultivating these friendships is an art which should not be overlooked by any professional salesman. In today's highly competitive business world there are many companies that offer the same products, services, prices and terms. And, with these things being equal or nearly equal, the sale often goes to the salesman who is on the most friendly terms with the buyer. Many salesmen, unfortunately, seem to shy away from developing friendships such as these because they feel the friendship would be insincere and devious. We say "unfortunately" because this is really a short-sighted view. *No business-related friendship can have a more solid foundation than one which is based on a salesman's genuine interest in his customer's welfare.*

If you are sincerely interested in the welfare of your customer, it could mean the beginning of a long and lasting friendship. On the other hand, there is nothing more disgusting than the salesman who tries to develop a friendship with a prospect merely to make an "extra buck." This type is soon discovered, and in the long run he never makes the big leagues. Always remember that you are probably not the first salesman to call on your prospect, and he has most likely met the deceptive "over-friendly" type.

The same rules apply when selling to friends and relatives. Never make a friend feel obligated to buy just because he is your friend. The salesman who prostitutes his friendships will eventually lose sales . . . as well as friends. When selling to friends, always be absolutely certain that they have a definite need for your product, and always keep their best interests at heart.

Handling the Old Customer

The best source for additional sales is the customer who is already "on the books." However, once you have created a satisfied customer, observe this caution: *Never take him for granted!* You do not own him; he doesn't have to buy from you; you do not have him in your hip pocket! *Never lose sight of the fact that your customer is a prime prospect for your competitors.*

Perhaps the Red Queen said it best when she advised Alice:*

> "Now, here you see, it takes all the running you can do to keep in the same place. If you want to get somewhere else, you must run twice as fast!"

Most likely, Lewis Carroll did not have the role of a salesman exactly in mind . . . but he nonetheless

*From *Alice in Wonderland,* by Lewis Carroll.

described very well the challenge faced by the modern salesman in his handling of the customer. It takes "all the running you can do" to get a customer. But once you have him, do not stop running! Instead "run twice as fast" to keep him satisfied. Every sale that is handled properly is an opportunity for future sales. Proper service and treatment will eventually mean bigger orders *and reorders* for tomorrow.

The progressive salesman also takes a *continuing* interest in his present customers. Thus, it is important for you to keep in touch with your customers; to call on them in person; to call them by phone; to drop them a note once in a while. For one thing, you should be making sure that all of them are using your product or service properly. If you sell merchandise at wholesale, see that your retailer accounts are displaying that merchandise properly; give the salespeople a few choice tips on how to sell it more easily; and make sure they never lose sales because you failed to give them enough support. And if you sell machinery, for example, make sure that your customer's workmen are using and maintaining it properly. In any field, continually offer special assistance to your customers.

It is also wise to show a *personal* interst in your customer—although you should be *discreet* about it. An anniversary card, birthday card or Christmas card shows that you are interested in him beyond your natural interest in making sales. This is the kind of thing that builds a solid customer-salesman relationship; it is what creates future orders and good will.

If you are a sales clerk in a retail store, remember that your job depends on the success of your store.

And the success of that store, in turn, is entirely dependent upon attracting enough customers through its doors to pay the expenses and show a profit on the owner's investment. *You* play a major role in this because you have direct contact with those customers. Their impression of the store is very closely tied to their impression of you. Always treat them courteously, alertly, and with a pleasant smile so that they will know you *want* to serve them. Be polite at all times, even with an irritable or tough customer. Keep in mind that the customer doesn't have to deal with you or your store—and there are many other stores and salespeople who are anxious to deal with them. You may be under the mistaken notion that you don't have to cater to your customers; that they must deal with you because they can't buy your product elsewhere; that they will have to pay a higher price if they go to your competitor; that your company's reputation allows you to take certain liberties; that your company's size gives it a certain edge—and so on. But don't think for a minute that customers will come to you in great numbers if you fail to make it pleasant for them to deal with you or if you fail to give them the kind of service and satisfaction they believe they are entitled to.

Repeat Orders

By and large, repeat orders come solely from completely satisfied customers. Ask an experienced salesman, and he will tell you that most often these repeat orders are also much larger than the initial sale. In many cases a buyer will place a small initial order because he wants a sampling before ordering "across the board."

Remember this advice always! It is your obligation to give your customer good service *merely because he is the customer.*

Any successful life insurance agent can tell you that "repeat business" usually becomes the most important part of his annual production after a few years in the field. Throughout the years a good client will add many policies to his insurance portfolio as his family and financial needs increase. Only by keeping his clients satisfied will the life agent realize the windfall of such repeat business.

A fringe benefit for a job well done is the additional business which will follow! And another fringe benefit is the referral business that a satisfied customer will give you. *The satisfied customer is by far the finest advertising in the world.*

III

MENTAL ATTITUDE: "THE POWER OF POSITIVE THINKING"

If one single element should be included in all "formulas for success," it should, without a doubt, be *proper mental attitude.* This is the common denominator among all successful men. *The power of positive thinking and success are synonymous.*

Study any successful man, and you will discover a man who thinks positively. All great men throughout history have had this trait. And if you are going to succeed in selling you, too, must have it. If you do not, you will be burdened with doubt, lack of confidence, hesitation, and all the negative thoughts which cripple a man's chance for success. Wipe away these liabilities; be a positive thinker.

Self-Image

"The building of sales confidence results from a conscious effort. A $50,000-a-year man doesn't just wake up and find himself such; it results from an accumulation of all the qualities which are developed by him through experience, training and believing in himself. He has to be able to look in the mirror and see a $50,000-a-year man before he can become one."*

Your entire life is influenced and—to a great extent—molded by your opinion of yourself. Throughout the ages, philosophers have told us "you *are* what you *believe* you are." If you look at yourself and think that you are honorable, conscientious, determined, courageous, capable and self-disciplined, then you have *positive* power. You have faith that you can do any job well. Without this faith and belief in yourself and your ability, you cannot make and carry out important decisions. In studying the lives of successful people you will see that they have a certain swagger, a certain aura of confidence, a sense of adventure and a strong sense of pride. They are people of action. They think positively, and they act positively. In other words, they have a positive image of themselves—and this is the self-image that they project to everyone around them. *Your* mental picture, too, is carried around with you wherever you go. It determines the kind of person that

*Herbert L. Greenberg, Chairman of the Board, Planned Equity Corporation. In 1972, Mr. Greenberg's company sold over $200 million of life insurance.

others perceive you to be; and, most importantly, it determines the kind of person you *actually are.*

You may have many special talents and capabilities, but if you allow your self-image to falter, then your gifts may waste away unused. You will begin "spinning your wheels," and your fear of failure will practically insure failure. The result is an inner battle that you wage against your fears and self-doubts; and this battle saps your energy. It drains your vitality. And the more you fight with yourself in this way, the more you see yourself as your own worst enemy.

What can you do to avoid getting into such a war with yourself? The answer is: *Think positively! Believe in yourself.* Believe in your chances for succeeding. Don't waste your energy or your time contemplating failure.

To understand a little more clearly how the power of a positive self-image works, let's take an imaginary case:

Let's say that John, a top executive with a salary in the $40,000 to $50,000 range, has been painting his house all day and is covered with paint from head to foot. (Of course, he doesn't *have* to paint his own house; but he *likes* to.) Dressed in old work clothes, he gives the outward appearance of a bum. At this point, he discovers that he's running low on paint, and so he hops into his car and goes to a nearby hardware store to pick up an extra can. When he arrives, looking shabby and dirty, a clerk walks briskly up to him and addresses him in the following manner: "Sir, may I be of assistance to you?"

Now, take another case. In this instance, a guy named Bill—who just happens to be John's identical twin—walks into the same hardware store, dressed in a similar manner, and is spoken to in this way: "Hey buddy, what can I do for you?"

Why was it that John was called "Sir" and was treated as though he were an important person, while Bill was addressed "Hey buddy"—as though he weren't worth the clerk's time? Since both men had identical physical appearances, there must have been something else that made John appear important and Bill insignificant. That "something else" was John's *self-image, which makes him feel important and which shows through to the people he comes in contact with.* His self-confidence has given him a certain posture, a certain way of walking, and a certain look in his eyes.

Bill's self-image, on the other hand, has made him come across as an unimportant nobody. Obviously, that's the way he feels about himself. And *it shows!*

In selling, just as in this little saga of John and Bill, there is no single force more effective than a salesman brimming with confidence and enthusiasm. The "I am important" attitude gets immediate attention from a prospective customer. Everybody enjoys doing business with the successful person—but few people want to associate with the unsuccessful. Imagine two salesmen walking into your office to do business with you. One is Willy Loman, from the play "Death of a Salesman." The other is Professor Harold Hill from "The Music Man." Is there any question as to which man is more exciting and interesting? Willy Loman drags his poor aching body through your door, while Professor Hill struts in with a spring to his step and confidence in his eyes. This self-image of importance creates excitement and immediate attention.

Likewise, the prospective customer immediately forms an opinion of *you* and of *your product* from the picture that your self-image gives him. If you impress him as being "important," then he will feel that you must have something important to sell. Nothing is more contagious than your enthusiasm. The buyer thinks: "It must be a good product; if it weren't, this salesman wouldn't be so sure of himself." On the other hand, the salesman with the poor self-image creates the corresponding impression. "Boy," thinks the buyer, "it must be murder to sell (whatever his line is); his product can't be very good!"

The salesman with the image of "the unimportant nobody" is, in effect, telling the buyer that he is a *dull salesman* from a *second-rate company* which sells *low-quality products* to only those buyers who have *poor credit ratings!*

Just as enthusiasm is contagious, so also is *hesitation.* The salesman who hesitates to close a sale will cause his buyer to hesitate to make up his mind. The salesman who "hems and haws" will most likely find his prospect wanting to vacillate and wait.

The "Mr. Milquetoast" salesman is also an easy person to refuse. His meek, faint-hearted personality invites procrastination on the part of the prospect, who will tend to put off his decision just as long as the timid salesman allows him to. The result usually will be *no sale!* On the other hand, if the buyer's impession of the salesman is that of an important man who can make important decisions, that buyer will usually react positively and make a decision.

Certain Signs of Poor Mental Attitude

There are certain physical and emotional traits that the salesman with the poor mental attitude usually possesses. His lack of enthusiasm will generally cause him to drag his feet, and he will not look you squarely in the eye. His lack of confidence gives him the appearance of the "beaten man." (If you close your eyes for a minute and think of an *un*successful person that you know, these physical appearances will become obvious.)

The negative mental attitude also usually causes him to be irritable, on edge, easily depressed and tired. He frets a great deal and feels that things are stacked against him. He complains that his territory is unproductive, his sales leads are poor, his product is not priced competitively. He feels that his sales manager has a grudge against him, his company is not giving him proper backing, he is unlucky, he gets all the bad breaks—and on and on. If this same man were to believe in himself and have faith in his abilities, he would have a new self-image and would see things in an entirely different light. With such positive forces pulling for him, he could then turn out to be an excellent salesman. His energy would pick up, and his confidence would motivate him to attain heights he had never believed possible.

How to Overcome the Fear of Failure

"Success is the ability to go from failure to failure without losing your enthusiasm." (Anonymous)

Real or imaginary, fear is insidious. It strips you of your motivation, it drains your courage, it stops you cold. The salesmen's graveyard is filled with would-be salesmen who were controlled by fear. The salesman who lacks faith in his ability, his product or his company hasn't got a chance for success from the very beginning. He not only doesn't belong in the sales field, he will also have a very difficult time fitting into *any* business enterprise.

When a salesman analyzes his fears and evaluates them intelligently, they usually evaporate—and he can then complete the tasks at hand. It is possible, of course, that lack of training and lack of product knowledge could rob a salesman of his confidence. Poor training can cause anyone to be disorganized and to waste time and energy. Not keeping up to date on the latest methods and developments in his field can make anyone lose confidence in himself and his company. The simple answer to this problem is to *get the necessary knowledge.* Dig a little harder. Study. Do research. And don't hesitate to tell your company when you feel that its training could be improved.

Rudyard Kipling said: "If you can force your heart and nerve and sinew to serve you until long after they are gone, and so hold on when there is nothing in you but the will which says to them 'Hold on!'—yours is the earth and everything that is in it." When the customer says "no" any salesman worth his salt knows that *this is when the sale begins.* The customer is merely saying: "I am not convinced; give me more information . . . give me a little better reason for buying." Instead of panicking, the salesman should recognize this signal and accept it for the great challenge that it is. It means that now is the time he must really convince the buyer. Now is the time to make the buyer *want* his product or service. This, after all, is what salesmen are for!

Obviously, you can't sell everybody, but if you accept "no" too easily, you're not apt to sell *anybody.* You must also have the ability to go from one "no" to the next without losing your enthusiasm. Never allow a "no" to carry over to the next presentation and possibly undercut your confidence. Clear your mind after each interview where you did not close the sale. Set up a "meditation room" in your mind to restore your enthusiasm. Make the necessary mental and emotional adjustments so that you will be in high gear for your next sales interview. By practicing this exercise before each sales presentation, you will gradually develop an ability to pick yourself up when you need it. Try practicing this mental exercise for the next month or two every time you have any doubts or fears. Do it when you feel tense after an interview. You will be amazed what it will do for your spirits and for your production quota. This mental interlude will relax you and help you unwind. When completely relaxed, you're less inclined to feel anxiety, strain, fear or anger. This will help you maintain your composure and restore your confidence. Then your next prospect will sense this positive power working for you. It will become contagious.

Psychological studies reveal that the chief cause of failure is the *expectancy* of failure. When you expect to fail and believe that you are going to fail, you will not disappoint yourself. By doubting, you develop a fear of attempting. Millions of individuals have lost chances at great achievements simply because they did not attempt what they could have accomplished. We respond to the demands that we make upon ourselves, and if we fail to be demanding upon ourselves we have no motivation to achieve. Make demands upon yourself! Set your sights and goals high, and then believe that you can accomplish them.

Positive thinking is so important that hundreds—perhaps thousands—of books have been written on the subject. It is so important that it is the basic philosophy of all religions. It is so important that this book brings up the subject only to make sure that you, too, are aware of its importance. To go into detail on this subject would require a book by itself. This chapter was included in our book because a book dealing with salesmanship would be incomplete without it—and if, by including it, we have stimulated your interest in the power of positive thinking, then it will have served its purpose. Perhaps you will want to read other books devoted entirely to the subject.

In the meantime, here are some other thought-starters that dramatize the importance of positive thinking:

"They are able because they think they are able."
(Virgil-*Aeneid*)

"Our doubts are traitors and make us lose the good we oft might win for fearing to attempt."
(Author Unknown)

A history of failure??? or a history of persistence???
   Failed in business in 1831
   Defeated for Legislature in 1832
   Second failure in business in 1833
   Suffered nervous breakdown in 1836
   Defeated for Speaker in 1838
   Defeated for Elector in 1840
   Defeated for Congress in 1843
   Defeated for Congress in 1848
   Defeated for Senate in 1855
   Defeated for Vice President in 1856
   Defeated for Senate in 1858
   ELECTED President of the United States in 1860 . . . ABRAHAM LINCOLN!

IV

WHY PEOPLE BUY

Why do people spend billions of dollars every year on goods and services? The answer is really very simple: Because they have *needs* and *desires*.

However, a need or a desire to own a product or command a service must be stronger than a buyer's natural instinct to hold on to his money. And, of course, it's the professional salesman's job to persuade the buyer to exchange his money for a product. In other words, the salesman must make people recognize needs and feel desires.

This facet of salesmanship is a vital part of your development if you wish to become a professional in the field of selling. You must understand the *motives that make people buy*. Without such an understanding, selling is merely a guessing game—a hit-or-miss proposition—and, at worst, a *con game*. Only when you understand the real motives that make people buy can you begin to employ the sophisticated, tested and scientific selling techniques that will make you a true professional.

The Buying Impulses

Nobody buys something for "no reason at all." Every time a purchase is made, the buyer is responding to a *motivation* of one kind or another. Perhaps his reasons for buying, in any given case, may seem unwise—even irrational—to others; but he nonetheless has a *reason*. These reasons for buying are what we generally classify as "buying impulses."

Psychologists usually divide the buying impulses into six categories, based upon their relationships to fundamental needs and desires:

1. *Security* (monetary gain, freedom from financial worry).
2. *Self-preservation* (safety and health—for self and family).
3. *Convenience* (comfort, more desirable use of time).
4. *Avoidance of Worry* (ease of mind, confidence).
5. *Recognition from Others* (social status, respectability, the wish to be admired).
6. *Self-improvement* (spiritual development, hunger for knowledge, intellectual stimulation).

Every time a person buys something, he is acting upon one or more of these six basic buying impulses.

To understand them a little better, let's look at a few examples of how these impulses relate to the more common and everyday types of purchases most of us make:

1. *Food, Clothing and Shelter.* Naturally, these are basic necessities of survival—and they should be placed at the top of the list. Every civilized person is a consumer of these goods and services, and the reason for purchasing such products is obvious . . . *self-preservation.*

2. *Other Necessities.* In our modern society, certain products have become "necessities"—even though our survival does not necessarily depend on them. Examples, for most of us, would include such items as an automobile, refrigerator, washer and dryer, telephone, bathtub and shower, and certain household furniture. Most of these things would not be considered "necessities" in most places throughout the world; but because of our high standard of living in the United States, even such products as television sets, wall-to-wall carpeting and draperies are considered by many Americans as being essential. To be realistic, however, we should place these products in the category of *convenience* purchases.

3. *Profit Gain.* Convince a man that he can make money with your product, and you will make a sale. The salesman calling on retailers, for example, must convince the retailers of the advantages of buying his product over that of his competitors. The retailer must be convinced that he can sell more of Brand X than some other brand—or that he can make more money selling it. The alert real estate salesman, likewise, points out to his buyer the high returns on the small investment in a property. The mutual fund sales executive outlines the growth patterns of the peak years of the stock market, and "on paper" shows his prospect a healthy profit. And the stockbroker may demonstrate the tax advantages of buying municipal bonds. These are just a few examples where *profit gain* is the chief motive in buying—and this motive, in turn, is related to the *security* impulse.

4. *Business Efficiency.* If you are an aggressive office machine salesman, you will point out the advantages of

owning an adding machine by convincing your buyer that your product can save time, eliminate errors, improve efficiency, and thus increase profits. Likewise, a cash register will increase efficiency and eliminate errors—so it, too, is an important aid to the operation of a profit-making company. Thus, as an office machine salesman, you would ordinarily be appealing to the buying impulses relating to *security, convenience,* and perhaps *avoidance of worry.*

A good example of top salesmanship is the office machine salesman who said to his prospect: "The paperwork pirate plunders profits! Any information written more than once costs you *time—and time means money!* Our highly accurate, photostatic copier will eliminate all errors and is simple to operate!" (He then, of course, went on to explain his copier in detail . . . and he got the sale!)

Another fine example is the case of "Mrs. Roberts." She said she wasn't interested in buying a dishwasher. But, after hearing a salesman describe the advantages of cleaner dishes, sanitary features, economics (fewer broken dishes), and so on, Mrs. Roberts began to change her mind. Then, when the salesman told her: "Perhaps the greatest advantage of all is the extra hour you'll save each day," Mrs. Roberts made her decision. She said, "Yes, I'll take it! I haven't been putting nearly enough time in on my rose gardening —and another hour a day is certainly worth it." (*You* can decide which buying impulse the salesman touched in this case.)

And then, we might also learn something from

the example set by the real estate salesman who was showing his prospect a new house in the suburbs. Noticing that the prospect had a set of fishing tackle in the back seat of his car, the salesman said: "Looks like you're a fisherman. By the way, have you ever been down to 'Barefoot Lake?' Where we have the summer cottages? The half-acre lots there are really nice. Most people are putting A-frame cabins on them . . . and everybody has his own private boat dock. Lots of terrific trout and walleye there, too!" (Obviously, this salesman had some lots at 'Barefoot Lake'—and he was talking to a prospect who liked to fish. Could there be any connection between this and the house in the suburbs—or was it simply a case of an alert salesman who was thinking of buying impulses?)

Emotional Needs

The six basic buying impulses involve both "rational" needs and "emotional" needs. People buy certain goods and services simply because it is necessary or practical to do so—because of *rational choice.* But people also buy many goods and services because of their *emotional drives.*

It is very important for the professional salesman to understand this distinction; to be able to recognize when he is dealing with rational buying situations and when he is dealing with emotional buying impulses.

Many times, of course, there is a very thin line between the two. And even if the primary sales appeal in a given case is aimed at an emotional need, the product may also have a quite rational or practical value to the buyer. The important point is that the salesman must know *which type of appeal* the buyer is most likely to respond to.

Let's examine some of the more common emotional needs and their relationships to the buying impulses:

1. *Security.* A basic need of human beings is to be *secure.* Products or services that can help satisfy this need may vary from seat belts to old-age pensions. Many people buy an automobile from one manufacturer as opposed to another, because they believe one manufacturer's car operates with *greater safety.* The need for security has made the life insurance industry one of the giants! The American public spends millions of dollars on preventive medicine every year. The United States Government spends *billions* of dollars on national defense. The entire world wants *security!* If your product offers a guarantee of security for the purchaser, make sure that you point out these features.

2. *Love.* People will do almost anything for their loved ones. Selling "security for one's family" has sold millions of life insurance policies. And, for example, the experienced educational salesman will say: "Mr. Jones, the entire future of your son depends upon your financing his education. Do you want your son to have a skilled profession such as our program offers? Do you want him to struggle for the rest of his life without the ability to support himself and his future family?" How many of us over-indulge our children with toys because of our *love* for them?

3. *The Sex Drive.* Sigmund Freud said that everything we do is based upon our *sex* drive! To discuss this opinion in detail would involve a separate book on the subject, and so we will mention only a few of the obvi-

ous products sold to appeal to the sex drive. Most cosmetics, for example, are purchased to make both men and women more appealing to each other. However questionable it may seem at times, our clothing is also designed to attract the opposite sex. The fashion experts often sell *sex* not *clothes*. *Playboy Magazine* has made a fortune in a very short time appealing to the sex drive. The movie industry sells sex on the screen! Some experts even claim that convertible automobiles appeal to men's sex drive!

4. *Recognition.* Another of our basic human needs is *to be recognized by others.* (Our egos crave for approval by our fellow man. America is a land of *status-seekers.*) The big luxury car is one of our foremost status symbols. How many people do you know who have bought homes they couldn't afford—just to impress others? This need for recognition sells diamond rings and mink coats. It is most evident that women buy mink coats for status when one views all the minks in Miami Beach on a hot night. People often build swimming pools in their backyards to impress others (some of these buyers don't even swim!). This need for approval supports resorts, country clubs, restaurants and—yes, even beauty parlors. Businessmen try to impress their clients with expensive suits, credit cards and limousines! Some people have their entire lives governed by the opinions of others—and all of us are greatly influenced by the need for recognition. Even the astute businessman will buy for recognition reasons. Most aggressive companies are very image-conscious today, and the smart salesman will realize this. "Mr. Williams," says the typewriter salesman, "notice the crispness that only an XYZ typewriter will have. You can always tell which companies go first-class by the quality of the typewriter they use. Every person receiving a letter from Williams and Company will be impressed with its appearance because you are using this typewriter. Every leading corporation in America

acknowledges this fact, and that's why they all use our equipment. It will build up your image to your most important people . . . the people you write to!"

5. *Pleasure.* Many purchases are made for just one simple reason—*Because it is fun!* The purchase of a theatre ticket or a ticket to see a sports event falls into this category. Millions of dollars are spent daily on outdoor games, sporting equipment, and other recreational products because *"they're just plain fun!"*

A Combination of Needs

A real problem is not only recognizing the needs of your customer, but also *combining his many needs* into your sales presentation. Discovering the customer's needs can be a *complex* problem which requires the finesse of the *professional* salesman. Only through experience and analysis can this talent be fully developed. It is, however, a worthwhile effort, because the rewards are great. Here are a few examples of buying situations where diffrent needs are *combined.*

1. *Life Insurance.* The most obvious appeal is *love* of *family.* Another would certainly be *security.* Possibly another would be *profit gain. Fear* may also play a decisive role in influencing the prospect. And even *recognition* can help sell insurance— since some people consider it "status" to own a lot of life insurance.
2. *Clothing.* Clothing, of course, is a basic need. But, again, the sex drive and the desire for recognition can be important influences in the decision about *what* clothes to buy. Even primitive tribesmen in the jungles wear certain paints and trinkets for *status.*

3. *Automobiles.* Today an automobile is certainly a *necessity* for millions of Americans. But, deciding on which style and which make to purchase can be a decision that is greatly influenced by needs for recognition, safety, pleasure and economy.

4. *Outboard Motor Boats.* Pleasure would seem to be the chief reason for buying a boat. But *status* can also be a reason.

5. *Diamond Rings.* A five-carat diamond ring would certainly seem to be purchased with *status* in mind. However, there can also be an element of pleasure involved—that is, the pleasure derived from the ring's beauty. And perhaps there is even a *rational* reason—a *hedge against inflation.*

6. *Automobile Tires.* Safety and economy are the prime reasons for purchasing auto tires.

7. *Pets.* The typical motives here include recognition, love, pleasure and—in the case of certain dogs—even security or safety.

8. *Homes.* The purchase of a home can include practically *all* of the basic impulses. First of all, a family must have *shelter.* A man may also buy a home for economic reasons—because real estate is a good investment or because it is more economical to own a home than to rent. A home will make certain people feel more *secure.* A man may buy a beautiful home because he loves his family and believes the environment of a beautiful home in a good neighborhood will play a major role in bringing up his children. The expensive home, of course, is always an excellent *status symbol* for those who seek *recognition.* (Read the real estate section of your newspaper, and notice how realtors appeal mainly to this need.) Finally, homes will give *pleasure* to their owners. A home with a built-in swimming pool and tennis court certainly will provide pleasure and sport for the family.

9. *Furniture.* Furniture is certainly a *necessity.* Expensive furniture also can be—and *is*—a *status symbol* to many people. Other people buy furniture mainly for the comfort or pleasure that it offers.

Wigs. There are several reasons why a woman would want to buy a wig. One is for sex appeal. Another is for status. Some women may rationalize and buy a wig for *economy* reasons because they believe, in the long run, it will be less expensive than going to the beauty parlor every week!

How to Discover a Buyer's "Real" Need

It is essential to discover the *real* need of your customer in order to create desire so that a decision to buy can be made. This is a talent that a salesman develops as he gains product knowledge and experience. Only through trial and error can some salesmen develop the knack of recognizing which buying impulse and which need he must appeal to. If you are conscientious, it will only be a matter of time until you acquire this *sales instinct.*

There will be many times when even the customer doesn't realize that his reason for buying is only an *excuse* and *not* the *real* reason at all! For example, a person may feel guilty about buying a house for its fancy address, and so he rationalizes and uses such excuses as "bought it for the children; it's such a good area for schooling!" Others will insist that "owning a Cadillac is economical," while the real reason they own it is for *status!* How many times have you heard a man claim that he bought his expensive golf clubs for "health reasons"—instead of admitting the fact that he just plain enjoys playing golf! In other words, some people feel *guilty* when they buy a product for *pleasure* or for *recognition*—and the salesman who recognizes this may save himself and his customers possible embarrassment.

Conclusion

The purchaser is always concerned with what he belives a product or service will do for him. He is interested in *how he will benefit. Remember this!* It is one of the most important lessons you will ever learn in studying to be a professional salesman. Regardless of what kind of goods or services you may be selling, you should gear yourself to think of your product not as a "thing" or a "process" but as a *benefit to your customer.*

One sales expert we visited with while researching this book likes to emphasize the *customer benefit concept* with this little illustration: He recalls going to a hardware store to buy an electric drill and being "sold" to the point of boredom on all the technical features and so-called "advanced" gadgetry of three or four different brands of drills. Finally, he interrupted the salesclerk and said: "Look, I don't care about the reverse upper wratchet-sprocket on the tidlum. All I want is some holes in my wall, and I want the best holes I can get for the least effort and the lowest price."

Think about that! The man didn't want a *drill*. He wanted *holes*. By the same token, you might ask whether a car salesman, for example, ever really sells *cars* . . . or whether he sells *transportation, pleasure, status, convenience, economy*—even *security* and *love.*

And you might consider whether a computer salesman really sells those wondrous machines with blinking lights and spinning discs—or whether he sells his clients *improved business efficiency, higher employee morale, better service to the client's customers, greater profitability*—or even earlier retirement and a luxury retreat in great trout country for the president and chairman of the client company.

So remember this! The customer is interested in the kinds of beneficial things that will happen to him when he buys your product. Of course, it is necessary for *you* to know where the wratchet-sprocket is, and whether your product has a tidlum . . . but most of your customers are more interested in "making holes."

Keep concentrating on those holes. Describe them; make them rounder, deeper and smoother. Make it easier and cheaper for your customer to have holes in his wall.

This is what the customer benefit concept is all about. It's why every professional salesman needs to understand the basic buying impulses and needs to be able to recognize them and make them work for him.

V

SELLING PATTERN

In developing any sales presentation there are actually *four phases* or *steps.*

STEP I—THE APPROACH: You must get the prospect's undivided attention. You won't sell a man who has something else on his mind.

STEP II—A FULL EXPLANATION OF THE PRODUCT: *Tell* him and *show* him what the product will do for him.

STEP III—CREATE DESIRE AND SHOW THE NEED: Make the prospect feel the need for your product, and make him *want to own it.* Show him what it will do for him.

STEP IV—THE CLOSE: Have confidence—and *ask for the order.* The first three steps are obviously wasted if the fourth step—the *close*—is not completed.

A sales presentation that covers these four steps and is presented dramatically is a *professional* presentation. It will produce *results.*

Remember: The way you say it (your delivery) is also very important. Present your idea dramatically, speak clearly, put pep and enthusiasm into your voice, and do not speak in a monotone. In other words, be an *actor.* A sale is like a performance on a stage. Your prospect is your audience.

Let's examine each of the four basic steps more closely.

The Approach

The approach is one of the most important factors in successful selling. Without an effective approach, you are in the same position as the football team who never gets the ball. (And, if a team doesn't get the ball, it can't score points.) Likewise, in sales, if you don't have proper exposure to your prospect, you cannot "score."

The first few seconds of your approach are the most important. Why? Because people often form snap judgments of other people, and you only have one chance to make that first impression a good one.

Remember (from Chapter IV) the office machine salesman who said, "The paperwork pirate plunders profits." He used a "headline" sentence; it only took him three seconds to say it; and he had the buyer's undivided attention. In other words, say something short and sweet; put a punch into it; get your prospect's attention—and you will be on your way to making a sale.

To prepare yourself, why not write down a few

short powerful openers and try them out. Be like a newspaper reporter: Figure out a few headlines to capture interest and hold your prospect's attention. And if these first few openers don't get you the proper results, then try a few more until you have several that really will work for you. You'll be amazed at the results you'll get.

Of course, you shouldn't use *trickery* in your approach. There is a difference between a "trick" and "trickery." Teachers use "tricks" to teach. Parents use "tricks" to get a child to take medicine or to eat his dinner. But "trickery" is *deception* and can only be used once. You never get another chance. Good approaches work without trickery. If you know your prospect's needs, you will find many good approaches. If you know your product and its benefits, then an easy and simple approach becomes obvious. For instance, the office machine salesman may say to his prospect, "Mr. Jones, you know speed and accuracy means more production at lower cost." By saying this, the salesman has made a short and snappy comment to arouse Mr. Jones' interest, and once he has Mr. Jones' interest, he can go on and elaborate.

Another good approach is the one used by a very successful adding machine salesman. He tells his prospect: "Eliminate the possibility of error and you will increase the opportunity for profit." In that first statement—which took only five seconds—he has aroused interest and won attention. It's easy! Try writing down such openers for your own selling situation. Go over the service plan or the product you sell, and see which features will arouse immediate attention and interest in just ten seconds.

"This floor polisher will do the job in half the time and eliminate back-breaking labor," says the door-to-door salesman—and the housewife invites him in for a demonstration.

"This electric mixer will mix a cake in one fifth the time and give you much smoother batter . . . It makes baking fun," says the salesman. Short, sweet and snappy; the housewife is all ears and eyes.

The salesman who is selling some type of *service* must be wary of his approach. He is selling *intangibles,* and he can't let his customer *feel* or *smell* or *see* his product. But if he can create a desire and make the prospect feel a need for his service, then he will make a sale. In other words, he must appeal to his prospect's buying impulses.

Service is easy to sell if you find out what your prospect needs. The linen supply salesman who is trying to sell the buyer in a large company his towel service, says: "I know you are interested in your employees' health." Thus, he makes a statement that can only receive a *yes* answer. And he gets the buyer's attention. "You are now using paper towels," he continues, "and the floors of your washrooms are all cluttered up with wet, unsanitary towels." The buyer becomes even more attentive because he has been in the washrooms himself, and has seen with his own eyes the scene that the salesman has just described. "Now," says the salesman, "We can put roll towels in each washroom, and you will have a clean, soft, fresh, sweet-smelling towel when you want it—and a cleaner, more sanitary washroom. Furthermore, a roll towel is more pleasant to use than messy paper towels, and it will make your employees a little happier. It will also cost you less than the paper towels, because they are being wasted."

What this linen service salesman has done is to paint a picture that his prospect can identify with. He has *shown* and *described* a situation relating to the prospect's needs—and thus he has appealed to a buying impulse—or several of them.

A Full Explanation of the Product

Once you have gotten in to see your prospect and you have his *undivided attention,* you then naturally show him exactly what *your product* will do for him. A good sales presentation should explain the benefits of your product in great detail so that no questions can be left in the prospect's mind. Whatever you may be selling, you must make sure that your prospect understands exactly what he is going to buy. If he does not understand how the product works, he will become confused and will not be able to make a decision. Many times, the confused customer, rather than admit his ignorance about your product, will create imaginary reasons why he does not want to buy.

Thus, it is very important that your presentation include a clear-cut description of your product and of what it will do for the prospect. It is also important that you show him *why* or *how* your product is better than your competitors'—and, of course, you must inform him about cost, terms and methods of payment or financing.

Finally, *ask for the order!*

Create Desire and Show the Need

After you have explained the benefits of your product, the real "selling job" is making your prospect *want your product more than he wants his money*. This is the part of selling that "sells the sizzle and not the steak."

Consider the successful automobile salesman who is trying to sell a man and his wife a new Oldsmobile "98" four-door hard-top. The salesman has been paying close attention to the husband's reactions to various remarks he has made, and he has also closely watched the wife's reactions. He has asked them in the course of the conversation their names and address, and thus he knows that they live in a fashionable suburb. Then he says: "Sir, just picture the admiration of your neighbors when they see you drive up in your new Olds. They'll be all eyes. And can't you just feel the smooth power when you step down on the gas to pass a slow-moving truck that's holding you back. Those power brakes will also give you an extra feeling of safety—along with the front and back seat belts—when you and the family are out driving. You owe that to your wife and children. And our new heavy shock absorbers give you the sensation of riding on a cloud. The power steering takes all the work out of parking for your wife—and I'm sure she'll appreciate that!"

After this, the prospect looks questioningly at his wife, and she looks wistfully at him.

The salesman then says: "Your car is two and a half years old and not equipped with power steering. I know it's hard work for your wife to squeeze into a parking space. Your old car also doesn't have the braking efficiency of power brakes, and the motor has lost some of its zip and smoothness. I'll never again be able to give you as much in trade as I can at this time. Would you like to drive the new one home this afternoon, while it's still light, so that your friends and neighbors can see it?" And she says, "I'm just crazy about it dear. Let's!"

This salesman has aroused his customers' desire by picturing the pride of ownership and the potential discomfort and unhappiness at *not* having the new car. He has given them a glimpse of the pleasure and satisfaction they will get out of the new car, with all of its power features. He has also appealed to an important buying impulse—their desire for admiration from their friends and neighbors. And, at the close, he has *asked for the order*.

The Close

The most important part of the entire sales presentation is the close—and, oddly enough, more salesmen are weaker here than at any other point in their presentations. This is ironic, because the first three steps of a presentation may be executed perfectly, only to be rendered irrelevant when the salesman can't close the sale!

The effective close must cover several key points. First, the salesman must show his customer *how* to buy. He must make it an *easy decision* for the customer to make. And, he must confidently assume that he has made the sale. Each of these points will be discussed in more detail in later chapters.

Too many salesmen work their hardest on the first three steps in selling and then put together a haphazard close; whereas the greatest amount of thought and concentration in developing a successful sales presentation should be in the closing.

Summary

Start now and make a list of "headline" approaches, and you will be on your way to making more and easier sales. Develop complete knowledge and understanding of what your product or service will do. Be equipped to answer all questions that may be asked of you. Study techniques on how to make your product sound very desirable. If necessary, use the dictionary and find descriptive words that paint vivid word pictures. If you miss in your approach and explanation of your product, you will not get a chance to *close* the sale. By the same token, if you cover the first three steps expertly and do not have an effective close, then the results will be the same—no sale.

VI

LET'S PUT SHOWMANSHIP
INTO YOUR SALESMANSHIP

Charlie Chaplin, screen star of the silent era, could express more joy and more pathos in pantomime than many of our great stars today can do with the aid of all the sound and graphics technology that Chaplin lacked. His secret weapon, *showmanship,* made him one of the greatest actors of all times.

Laurel and Hardy could also make their audiences roll in the aisles with just an expression.

Jackie Gleason, one of the great comedians of the TV era, can express joy, anger, sorrow, stupidity or timidity, and can tell a story with just a change of facial expression and the use of his hands.

Shirley Temple—when she was captivating American audiences as a child star—could bring tears to your eyes with just a certain look.

When Phil Silvers would light up a cigarette in the Camel commercial, he would take a deep drag, his

burns silently without warning until it
e tells his story—with proper dramatics
get higher and higher and hotter and

insurance salesman rings up a sale by
d picture of a grieving widow with three
n left penniless by an inconsiderate hus-

death is when you and your family slowly
e savings melt away like a piece of butter
skillet," says the dynamic health and acci-
n. "When your savings are wiped out and
ng stroke will not allow you to return to
ill you do to provide your loved ones with
o pay the bills that keep piling up?"
salesman sees the impact of his imagery
k in his client's mind, he continues: "This,
is living death—which is worse economi-
r family than actual death. This is a time
readwinner has no income but is still a
with *heavy medical bills!* Now let's see if you
for this policy while you are still fortunate
have good health!"
ever you speak, fortify your words with *ges-*
cial or body. Practice in front of a mirror to
your personality with meaningful facial ex-
Nobody likes to listen to a person with a
face, and there is absolutely no excuse for a
to have one. Facial expressions can put the
rommph" into your words, and—in many in-
can *replace* words. The right smile at the right

eyes would half close, his head would be tilted back, a satisfying smile would appear, he would slowly exhale, and the smoke would come out as though he hated to part with it. You were shown the *pleasure* in smoking Camels. Phil made you want to try one!

Showmanship is salesmanship at its best! Showmanship is a vital part of selling, and it must be incorporated into your sales presentation. Add the *extra punch* of showmanship to your presentation, and your sales are bound to soar! Remember: *Your customer is your audience.* It doesn't matter whether you are selling one person or a group of people. The professional salesman knows how to set the stage and give a performance that will guarantee results.

Franklin D. Roosevelt was another man who certainly knew how to use showmanship to the hilt in his "fireside chats" with the nation. Winston Churchill also performed beautifully during World War II. His image is now immortalized with a big cigar in one hand, and another hand waving "V" for victory. Of course, it's too bad that Hitler possessed it—this same quality of showmanship. Unfortunately, it was one of his greatest assets. Unshaven Fidel Castro knows all about it, too. And how can we ever forget Nikita Krushchev pounding his shoe at the United Nations! The brilliant John F. Kennedy was so aware of the importance of showmanship that he was professionally coached before he debated with Richard Nixon on television—and history gives credit for his television performances during these debates as the deciding factor that won him the office of President of the

United States. Ex-actor Ronald Reagan certainly used his ability as a showman in winning his election as Governor of California—and in becoming a strong national political figure.

These are just a handful of cases in politics where showmanship has been used. In fact, it's actually hard to come up with the name of any high-ranking politician who *doesn't* employ showmanship. (Try "grading" the candidates on this score in the next election that comes along.)

Since showmanship is such a powerful influence over people, shouldn't *all salesmen* take full advantage of it? After all, selling is the art of *influencing*—so it would be foolhardy to neglect the use of such a mighty tool. Start immediately: Put showmanship in *your* selling!

Why Showmanship?

Good showmanship has many functions in the selling field. Most importantly, *it gives you a captive audience.* Without the undivided attention of your customer, you certainly cannot reach your peak of effectiveness in selling. Many times a customer seated directly across the desk from a salesman will not hear a word that he utters! A customer may give a salesman the courtesy of allowing him to go through his sales presentation, but this does not necessarily mean that the message is getting through. Without proper showmanship, the customer's mind can fade a thousand miles or a thousand years away! *In short, a prospect*

time can show approval or disapproval better than words. A certain smile can say: "Are you kidding? You're out of your mind if you pass this up," (which is something you wouldn't dare come right out and say). (Picture Jack Benny's expressions, and you'll get the point.)

Another thing—there is no law that a salesman can't use his arms and the rest of his body when he is talking! Never be afraid to wave your arms, shrug your shoulders, pound a desk, or even jump up and down to make a point! There is no rule of etiquette that says a salesman can't talk with his hands. Don't ever be afraid of being accused of "talking like a foreigner with his hands." Use every available tool you've got to get a point across. If you do not take advantage of facial expressions and body movements, you are no better than a tape recorder.

It goes without saying that "how you say it is sometimes more important than *what* you say!" If you want to be a good showman, learn to speak *distinctly* and use proper *pronunciation*. Learn to speak *clearly* and *precisely*, so that your listener doesn't have to strain to understand you. Learn to vary your voice . . . high and low . . . fast and slow. The quickest way to put a customer to sleep is to speak in a monotone! Speak low at a whisper . . . and loud with a roar. Talk slow when emphasizing an important point. Increase your rate of speech when going over minor points. Talk loud and bold at times to emphasize your complete confidence in the strong points. At times, you should lower your voice to convey "confidential" information

—as though you were telling a secret. Lower your voice if you want to give a dramatic effect to what you are saying. You don't have to be an actor to dramatize important points. It's easy! The rule of thumb is *variety*. Don't bore your listener with a steady, monotonous presentation that *drags* and *drags* and *drags*.

Study the Pros

Learn from the "champs." If you want to be a good showman, you can obtain a free education from what you see and hear on television and radio—on the commercials, as well as the programs. The finest selling in America is being done with professional showmen every ten or fifteen minutes on the commercials that you see on television. The sponsors have spent much time and large amounts of money to perfect this medium of advertising—and it is worth your while to pay close attention to these professional presentations.

Don't ever forget it: The main function of all advertising is *selling!* Study the professional techniques; learn showmanship from the experts.

Notice how the TV commercials emphasize the superiority of their product over the competition's.

Palmolive soap commercials are good examples: A beautiful movie star tells you that she wouldn't think of using any other soap but Palmolive. Her beauty is an envious example of what many women, consciously or subconsciously, want to look like . . . perfect skin, beautiful complexion, and so on. Then, the girl in the commercial demonstrates how to massage Palmolive lather into the skin. This demonstration is superb showmanship.

Notice, also, how the hair-care and razor blade commercials use showmanship to sell *men!* They *tell* you and *show* you proof of their "superiority."

Another way to learn more about showmanship is to observe your *peers.* Ask the leading salesman of your company if he wouldn't mind having you spend a day or two with him. Tell him: "I want to see a real pro in action"—and, chances are, he will be so flattered that he'll be delighted to take you along. It's a sure bet that you'll be investing your time wisely and will pick up some good tips on salesmanship and showmanship.

The next time you go shopping, or the next time a salesman calls on you . . . study the techniques that they use. You are bound to learn something from each one. Notice the differences in the presentations of the life insurance salesmen who use showmanship and the ones who don't. Notice how the leading car salesmen use showmanship. Whether you are buying a suit, a TV set, or a set of encyclopedias, look for and study the different methods of showmanship used by those salesmen. Never be ashamed to borrow ideas from people in your profession. It's a perfectly legitimate way to build your own skills.

There are also free lessons around that will teach you showmanship in your everyday normal living. Study and observe what you see and hear. *It doesn't cost anything.*

The Showman Gets the Buyer in the Act

"Now follow the bouncing ball . . ." *"Sing along with Mitch."* *"Will somebody from the audience please step forward."*

What these quotes add up to is: *Getting the buyer into the act. Audience participation* is another way to describe it. Instead of just observing, the audience is also *doing.* The fastest way to get the complete and undivided attention of your customer is to *have him participate in the sale.* Customer participation is one of the most effective methods of selling.

The smart educational salesman may also appeal to the parents' love of their child as he explains the difference his product will make in the child's future earning potential.

Paint a dramatic picture in the mind of the emotional buyer, and a sale can be made! *Showmanship* is the most effective tool a salesman can use to create emotion.

How to Be a Showman in Selling

To use showmanship, you must appeal to your customer through his *senses.*

The two most important senses are *sight* and *hearing.*

But don't overlook *touch, smell* and *taste.* Hand an article to your customer and let him "play" with it. Tell him to smell its fragrance—"Here, I want you to taste this." Smack your lips and say, "Isn't that delicious cheese?" Did you ever notice how candy stores lure you in with the sweet aroma of their chocolates and fudges? Also, the nut store with its inviting aroma makes it hard for a passer-by not to stop in. And the tempting smell of the bakeshop makes you spend your money quicker than any sales talk could! (There are new car dealers who actually spray the interior of an automobile which has been used as a demonstrator . . . *to give it the smell of being brand new!*)

Use your imagination, and there will be no limit to the showmanship that you can achieve in making a sale. As Napoleon said: "The human race is governed by its imagination."

People like to handle items themselves. They like to play with gadgets . . . turn them on and off. *Invite them to do so.*

"Here, try it, see how easily it operates. Press this for 'on' and that for 'off' ".

In other words, have your customer be part of your presentation. His concentration and curiosity will keep him active, and you will have his complete attention.

The Sheaffer pen salesman calls on the buyer of a large store and shows him the new feather-touch ball-point pen. The buyer says, "I am completely loaded. We have too many pens in stock right now. I am not interested!" With a pleasing smile, the salesman says, "Wonderful, but none are like ours. Let me show you how easily this pen writes on contact with a writing surface." While he is talking, he takes an egg out of a box and peels part of the shell (about the size of a dime) off the tip and writes the buyer's name on the soft tender membrane. "See that! See how easily it writes without pressure. The slightest bit of pressure would surely have broken the thin membrane!" The salesman then pulls out a jar from his sample case and breaks the egg into the jar to prove that the egg was not hardboiled. "I'll bet you thought I was using a hardboiled egg," he says.

This kind of showmanship is one of the things that makes the difference between a *professional* salesman and the non-professional.

The smart clothing salesman says to his customer: "Feel this material. It's soft, and yet it has body. It will hold a crease in the dampest climate." If the customer's wife is with him, the salesman may turn to her and say: "I want you to feel this material." In other words, he gets *her* into the act, too. He gets her on *his side.* He then proceeds: "Now watch this," taking the sleeve and twisting it over and over until he has a tight braid. "See the abuse this material will take! Naturally, you'll never do *this* to the garment, but it is expertly woven to take this kind of abuse." As he releases the sleeve, and it unwinds like a spring, he adds: "Notice, not a wrinkle." This, again, is smart *showmanship.*

A large midwestern department store was introducing a new floor polisher, and had advertised it in the local newspaper, telling people to come in and see a remarkable demonstration. The store had a platform with floor covering set up, and a very pretty model in an evening gown putting wax on the floor with a mop and then polishing the floor with ease by using the electric waxer. The demonstration made the task look simple enough for any child to do. Next, a child of ten years was picked from the crowd, and she did the other side of the floor. The store sold out of polishers the first day! (Another case of excellent showmanship.)

A saleslady in another department store was selling alarm clocks. The prospect said she didn't want an electric alarm because she didn't have an outlet in her bedroom. The saleslady wound up a "Baby Ben" alarm clock and handed it to the customer, saying: "Listen, you can't even hear it tick." The customer placed the clock next to her ear and listened with amazement. The saleslady then said, while winding up the clock, "This 'Baby Ben' will *not* keep you awake at night listening to the monotonous tick." As she wound the alarm and set it, she added: "Even the alarm was purposely made subdued and gentle so that you will not wake up with surprise." She then had the customer push the lever to see how easily the alarm could be turned off. As the customer did this, the saleslady said: "Now push the lever marked 'soft or loud' and notice what a difference there is. Whatever sound suits you best, you can adjust for your personal pleasure." She then smiled and said: "Would you like it gift-wrapped?" (This is the kind of showmanship that allows the customer to participate. It is a tested way of increasing your sales production.)

These are just a few examples of salesmanship that *brings the customer into the act.* Think of the times when, for example, you went shopping for a car, and the *good* salesman let you drive the demonstrator and try out the new gadgets. Naturally, the good TV sales-man will also let you adjust the color controls while he is demonstrating the performance of the set. And a good furniture salesman will have you sit in the com-fortable chair; while some will even have you *lie down on the new mattress!* Finally, the good electric razor salesman will go so far as to let you shave with the demonstrator.

This type of showmanship is the most convincing of all salesmanship because it proves to the buyer how he can benefit from the sale.

Conclusion

It has often been said that there is a great similarity between *selling* and *acting.* The greater show that you put on as a salesman, the better results you will get. Just as the professional *actor* rehearses time and time again to achieve perfection, so also should you as a *salesman* practice your sales presentation. With imagination, all salesmen should be able to in-corporate showmanship in their sales presentations. Concentrate on this, and watch your sales soar!

Showmanship in selling is salesmanship at its finest!

VII

APPEARANCE AND SALES ETIQUETTE

Sometimes the most obvious is overlooked. It would be foolish to take for granted that all salesmen automatically possess the proper appearance and sales etiquette. The role of the salesman is similar to that of an ambassador or a diplomat. With this thought in mind, the professional salesman must be very diplomatic in his appearance and actions. Committing an error in either can mean the loss of a sale! If you hope to rise to the top in the sales field, it is very important that you acquire polish and good sales manners.

Appearance

In the selling field—as in all walks of life—*first impressions* are of major importance. Perhaps they are even *more* important in the selling field because a poor first impression can cost you money! It can be not only your first, but also your last, chance to make an impression. Usually, once the door is closed you don't get in again. The most important rule to remember is: Make absolutely sure that your *appearance* is not offensive to anyone. This is such a simple and obvious rule that many salesmen overlook it. You cannot afford to be offensive to a prospective customer. This rule applies to your appearance from the time you leave your home in the morning till the time your day is ended.

Number One: Your Car

A smart salesman should be aware of his appearance at all times. When he pulls into the parking space in the front of the store, or into the parking lot, his prospect may be watching him. He never knows who may be observing him, so he must be on guard at all times. Even the type of car you drive may make a difference. A car in a poor physical condition (with dented fenders or rusty chrome) certainly connotes a down-and-out salesman. Or you might consider that the convertible will offend some types of customers— and may even create the impression of a "playboy" type of salesman. The same would apply to the salesman in the sports car. Many an order has been torn up when the customer saw that the salesman was driving a *foreign* automobile. When times are tough, and "Buy American" campaigns are the topic of conversation, an imported car can anger a buyer and sway him in favor of your competitor. The authors discovered one instance where a steel salesman asked his customer to lunch after making a big sale. The salesman insisted:

"Be my guest, I want to give you a ride in my brand new car. I'll take you out to my club." When the steel executive saw his new car—a brand new foreign model —he fumed, "Not only will I not eat lunch with you, but I want that order cancelled immediately. I don't do business with people who buy imported cars!" The sale *was* cancelled—and there was nothing the salesman could do to change his customer's mind. This, of course, is an extreme case, but the professional salesman might well consider such possibilities.

Another extreme example involving the type of car a salesman drives is dramatized in the case of one of the country's top encyclopedia salesmen who rode in a chauffeur-driven Rolls Royce in Rye, New York. He would have the chauffeur pull up in front of the customer's house, ring the doorbell, and tell the housewife that a top executive of the company wished to discuss some ideas with her about encyclopedias. Where other salesmen could not get their foot in the door in this fashionable neighborhood, this particular salesman made such a strong impression that he was enthusiastically greeted by practically everyone. Had he *not* played his role to the hilt—or had he perhaps driven a big medium-priced automobile himself (without the chauffeur), the effect would have been quite different. Perhaps he *was* a little "devious"—but, then, remember our previous chapter on "showmanship."

Naturally, your authors are not suggesting that you have to drive an expensive car to be successful— but the important lesson to remember is: *Even your car will leave an impression.*

Number Two: The Proper Way to Dress

Common sense would seem to indicate that all salesmen know how to dress—but the evidence is not that convincing. There are simply too many sloppy, improperly dressed salesmen around for us to justify such an assumption. Again, the professional salesman cannot afford to dress in a manner which will be offensive to his customer. For example, "loud" or garish clothes are not only in poor taste, but also tend to irritate the people you call on. Many customers have formed unfavorable opinions about salesmen walking into their stores with loud sports jackets or suits. The typical reactions (even in the "mod" era of today) might stamp the "loudly" dressed salesman as a fly-by-night or a tasteless joker. What a poor way to start off a sale! Why have two strikes against you before you enter the door? If you like to wear loud clothes, that's fine, as long as you do it in your leisure time. But not for business. Conservative clothes have never offended anybody, so why take chances and rub somebody the wrong way by the way you dress?

Let's apply the law of averages to this phase of selling, and remember: Spectacularly or shabbily dressed salesmen will lose a certain percentage of sales for no other reason than their appearance. It may be a matter of *mistrust* or *disgust*. The effect on sales is the same.

A salesman should always wear a tie. (Stripes, plain, or neat prints are recommended—nothing "loud"). His suit should always be well pressed—with no buttons missing! He should always keep his shoes well polished and in good repair (avoiding the run-down-heel look). He should never pull out a dirty handkerchief or one with a hole or ragged edge. And a frayed shirt is a sign of hard times.

The salesman who dresses immaculately creates the image of an efficient, well-polished and confident individual. Shouldn't *you* have this working in *your* favor?

Another important requirement is to always maintain your *dignity.* Regardless of the weather, never call on a prospect carrying your jacket, or with your tie loosened and your shirt collar unbuttoned. *Dignity inspires confidence!*

Naturally, when traveling out-of-town, make sure that you take the necessary amount of clothes so that you are always freshly groomed. It is always better to take along *too many* clothes than not enough! Also, allow for enough clothes to take care of an emergency, such as a spilled drink, a spot on your tie, or a cigarette burn. When seeing a customer twice in the same week, it is also wise to wear different clothes on each occasion. Let him know that you have more than one suit! Everyone likes to do business with a *successful* person. Success breeds success.

Number Three: Personal Hygiene

Just as important as the clothes you wear is the clean body that they cover. It is important to be clean-shaven at all times (unless, of course, you sport a stylish and neatly trimmed mustache or beard). It's also critical that you guard against offensive odors. You can ill afford to offend your customers because of body odor or bad breath. The drug stores are well supplied with excellent mouthwashes and deodorants which give you protection. Naturally, your hair should always be combed, and don't give the impression you can't afford a haircut! (Even if you wear your hair modishly long, there's a difference between a stylish trim and pure neglect or sloppiness!) It's ridiculous to let these little things interfere with your chances of making a sale—but, nonetheless, they *will* sabotage you if you are not careful!

Sales Etiquette

The simplest sales etiquette rule to remember is: *Always use your best manners.* It certainly doesn't cost anything to be polite and agreeable, and courtesy pays tremendous dividends. *Everybody likes to do business with a gentleman.* No matter what type of manners your customer *displays*, show him that *you* are a *gentleman* . . . even if it hurts! Even if you don't like him, at least *act like you do.* This is not being *insincere* . . . it's just plain *good business.*

There are many times when you will approach a prospect and he will display deplorable manners. Don't let this affect *your* behavior. Your first reaction may be a desire to give him "a dose of his own medicine"—but this will accomplish nothing. It will merely make him feel justified about the way he treated you in the first place, and things will get continuously worse. By rising to the occasion and keeping calm, your good breeding will catch him off-guard. Then you—and not he—will control the situation. Chances are great that you will eventually win him over and gain a friend!

Certainly good manners have never hurt a salesman's chances of success.

Some Good Rules on Sales Etiquette are:

1. Never chew gum or eat candy or snacks when talking to a customer.
2. Never smoke while making a presentation (unless the prospect himself is smoking and invites you to do so). Not only is smoking distracting while you are selling, it is quite offensive to non-smokers!
3. Never be late for an appointment. There is absolutely *no* excuse to keep somebody waiting—except death or accidents—and in cases like that, *call* him.
4. If you can't keep an appointment, have the courtesy to call and let the other party know.
5. Always give a warm greeting.
6. Avoid off-color jokes . . . and, especially, ethnic jokes.
7. Avoid conversations on religion, politics and race.
8. Never "go over somebody's head" . . . (always make sure that the man you are talking to is the right man who can make the decision to buy).
9. Always be friendly. Your *telephone* voice can also give an impression of friendliness. Be aware of this; it makes a difference! Put a smile on your lips and in your voice—and make sure your eyes are smiling.

10. If selling a man and wife together, never ignore either one of them. Always bring the wife into the conversation. You never want somebody to think you are snubbing them.

11. Never pull at your clothes, tap your fingers, tap a pencil, keep scratching or figiting, etc. This makes your prospect nervous and ill-at-ease.

12. Never lean on a door, a counter, desk, etc. Stand up straight. Be—and *act*—relaxed.

13. Always look your customer directly in the eye.

14. Never ignore a question. Give direct answers. There is no such thing as a bad question (or a stupid one).

15. Never show impatience. This applies to *all* phases of selling—from the reception room to waiting for a decision to be made in the close of a sale.

16. Never give an insincere compliment. Insincere flattery is too obvious. It is *not* really difficult to find something sincere to say.

17. Always show interest in your customer. Be a *good listener.*

18. Always take off your hat when you enter a house or a business establishment.

19. Never force yourself upon a customer at a time when it is inconvenient for him to talk to you. Remember: It's *his* privilege to talk to whomever he chooses.

20. Always thank your customer for his time when you have finished your presentation or your sale. This is a way of letting him know you believe his time is valuable.

Smile "If It Kills You"

A pleasant smile is one of the most valuable assets a person can possess in the selling field—or in *any* walk of life. Smiling is not just a movement of the lips.

It has to come from deep down inside you. It should be sincere. You can always tell a *real* smile by gazing into the eyes. When you muster up a genuine smile, your eyes and your lips smile at the same time. A warm friendly smile will open many doors.

The Value of a Smile

It costs nothing, but creates much.

It enriches those who receive, without impoverishing those who give. It happens in a flash, and the memory of it sometimes lasts forever.

None are so rich that they can get along without it.

It creates happiness at the home; fosters goodwill in business; and is the countersign of friends.

It is rest to the weary, daylight to the discouraged, sunshine to the sad, and nature's best antidote for trouble.

Yet, it can't be bought, begged, borrowed, or stolen—for it is something that is no earthly good to anybody until it is given away.

And . . . if we are too tired to give you a smile, may we ask that you leave one of yours . . . for nobody needs a smile as much as those who have none left to give.

Author Unknown

Conclusion

Don't for a moment underestimate the importance of proper appearance and sales etiquette. Without them, the role of the salesman will be unbearably rough. Make good grooming and charming manners a part of you . . . a part that comes as naturally as breathing. These habits are so easy to incorporate that it is a sin not to take advantage of them. You will also discover as a bonus value that they make your work much more pleasant and productive—and that mere living will be happier!

Remember: *A gentleman gets treated like a gentleman.*

VIII

THE TIME ELEMENT

"Time Is Money" (Bulwer-Lytton-Money)

The value of a salesman's *time* is practically immeasurable. Yet, oddly—and unfortunately—many salesmen seemingly place little value on this precious resource.

The *professional* salesman, however, must fully understand the importance of time. He must have the utmost *respect* for it . . . he must *cherish* it!

Measuring Your Time

As a salesman, of course, you are usually paid for *results*—not for "hours on-the-job." But, don't forget that results take time to accomplish. Results depend upon your ability to use time productively.

Even though you are not paid by the hour, it is still possible to determine the approximate value of your time in terms of "so much per hour." To do this, simply divide your annual income by the number of hours you worked last year. In order to determine the number of hours you worked, multiply 50 weeks—allowing for vacations—times the amount of hours in your "average" week. After making such a calculation, some salesmen will discover that they are averaging more than $100 an hour—while others will find that they would be better off if they worked on an assembly line and got paid by the hour! It's too bad that many salesmen would be *ashamed* to know how little they earn for the hours they spend at their jobs. If you want to avoid such an unpleasant shock at the end of the year, then you ought to begin thinking right now about how productively you are using your time.

Most salesmen like to say: "My time is my own." In other words, there is nobody watching over you to supervise your working habits. There is no boss to tell you what to do at any given moment. There is no time clock to determine when you start the job or when you finish for the day. You are on your own!

Of course, if this is the case, then it's up to you to take full advantage of each hour so that you get the maximum benefit out of each day. With this in mind, you will discover that even those little coffee breaks can cost a lot of money!

You must learn to appreciate the full value of your time. The first step is to respect every one of those precious minutes—because those minutes make up the hours and days.

In order to begin properly measuring and organizing your time, let's first find out which portion of your time is the most valuable. The obvious answer is: the hours when you are able to make calls on your prospects. If you are selling to restaurants, for example, the best selling hours would be in mid-morning and mid-afternoon, while the worst time to see your customer would be during mealtime when he is simply too busy to see you. Likewise, if you sell to an industry where the executives work weekdays from 9:00 to 5:-00, then your most valuable time during the day would be beween these hours. However, you should always allow time for your prospect to get organized in the morning, and you should make sure your sales presentation does not run past 5:00, unless the prospect specifies differently. In the same way in which you gauge the value of different times of the day, you can also determine which days of the week, which portions of the month, and which seasons of the year are most valuable for calling on certain customers. In the clothing business, for example, the back-to-school season is the busy time of year—so it would be hard for the wholesale clothing salesman to make sales presentations at this time. Likewise, a jeweler is too busy to see just before Christmas.

Salesmen in fields like insurance or mutual funds are fortunate because they call on virtually all types of clientele whose businesses and jobs vary like day and night. Consequently, they can set up their work day with prospects who can be contacted throughout the day (and evening too). The seasoned life insurance agent, for example, knows which prospects can be seen during the morning, afternoon and evening. For example, Joe Joseph, the foreman at the local factory, can't be contacted until 4:30 p.m. at his home. Bill Williams, who owns a delicatessen, is a good mid-morning or mid-afternoon call. Bob Roberts, who owns Roberts' Jewelry, shouldn't be called on during the Christmas season. Dick Richards, who is a manufacturers' rep. should only be contacted in the evenings . . . or perhaps he would make a good luncheon appointment. Some mediocre agents complain that they don't have bankers' hours (9:00 to 4:00), while the top life underwriters believe themselves lucky to have a sales position where they can get sales-exposure during the day and night!

It's up to you to know the best time and the proper season to call on your customers. In other words, it's up to you to plan and organize your time in relation to your customer's time. It's up to you to determine when your most productive hours, days, weeks and seasons are likely to come.

Planning Ahead

Once you have determined what your most valuable hours or seasons are, you must then plan to take the fullest advantage of them. You must organize and concentrate your efforts so that every one of those precious moments will count for something. Of course, it's humanly impossible to get 100 percent productivity out of *every* moment. But, if you don't set yourself that "impossible" target, you're not likely to even get close to it.

Your high-potential selling times should always be concretely planned in advance—never left to chance. *Tonight* is the time to plan *tomorrow's* day. *This season* is the time to plan *next season's* calls. Too many salesmen idle away too many precious minutes and hours "in the field" trying to decide who to call on next. It's easy to pull off the road and drop in at the nearest coffee shop (or bar) and pass away some "think time." It's easy to delude yourself into believing that these wasted moments are sorely needed "breathers"—that they are necessary for "recharging your batteries," or that they are "planning periods." Undoubtedly, everyone *does* need such "breathers"—such idle moments—but, if you are going to be a *professional* salesman, you must learn how to pace yourself, so that you can enjoy those much-needed "breathing spaces" at times when they are less costly. Your *real* planning should be done *before you go into the field.* And, if you have done a good job of planning and organizing, you'll find that there are very few "unassigned" moments during your peak selling time.

There are many salesmen who have the *ability to sell* but who lack the *ability to organize their time.* This is ironic, because it is *not* really difficult to organize your time effectively. There is no exotic expertise required. You don't need a college degree to do it. And you shouldn't even need a "sales training" course to learn it. All it really requires is *self-discipline* . . . a recognition of the *need* to do it, and a *determination* to go ahead and do it! It can be as simple as spending an hour or two on a Sunday evening to review your next week's appointments and look for unused or uncommitted time.

It can be as simple as keeping a clean and legible appointment book—or a "diary" of sales calls. It can also mean intelligent planning of travel routes—developing itineraries to give you the widest coverage of your territory in the shortest amount of travel time. It can be a matter of sorting, filing, and keeping at your fingertips a list of new leads—to be checked out whenever you find yourself with those idle and tempting "coffee-break" moments. In other words, it's not much more than a *common-sense* outlook on your business life. It's a matter of deciding whether you are really a professional at what you're doing, or whether you are simply a hit-and-miss salesman, between jobs, treading water while you wait for the big windfall from the skies.

Perhaps a few more practical tips will help get our point across:

Remember—every evening of your working time you should review and—if necessary—readjust your schedule for the next day. Possibly, one of your appointments for tomorrow was cancelled through a phone call from the prospect late this afternoon. This could leave a big—and *costly*—gap in tomorrow's agenda. You should ask yourself, *tonight*, "Who will I call in the morning to try to fill this dead time?"

Even if there have not been any definite cancellations in tomorrow's schedule, you should nonetheless consider the possibility that by morning there *will* be. In other words, always allow for the unexpected. It's not even a bad idea to plan more calls than you can possibly make in a day—just to cover the eventuality that some of your planned calls won't materialize. (Obviously, we're not talking here about situations where you have concrete appointments with customers, since you would never want to make appointments that you know you can't keep.)

As we mentioned a few paragraphs back, you may also find it very useful to work out travel routes or itineraries in advance. Depending upon the type of selling you do, this can mean a huge difference to you, not only in terms of travel expenses, but also—and more importantly—in terms of the effective use of your available selling time. It's a very *un*professional salesman who wastes his time running from one end of town to the other and then right back again to where he started. (Yet, isn't it surprising how many salesmen actually do this!) The point is that you, as a salesman, are not paid by the mile. You are not a cabbie or bus-driver. And your performance is certainly not gauged by the number of miles you cover. Companies don't make money that way. In fact, most well managed companies make it a point to establish sales offices in cities that are centrally located to their market areas. For example, Columbus (Ohio) is located just about in the center of the state—within three hours' driving time of almost any other spot in Ohio. As might be expected, Columbus is the site of many, many sales headquarters for companies that sell throughout the state. Other good examples include such cities as Indianapolis, Harrisburg (Pennsylvania), Atlanta and Denver.

To summarize the subject of *planning your time:*

Remember—there are only so many hours in a day and so many days, weeks and months in your active selling career. So, it only makes good sense to get the most you can possibly get out of this precious time you have available! If you are going to be a *professional* salesman you cannot afford the enormous waste that so many *semi-pros* are guilty of through poor planning, disorganization and negligence.

The "Slack" Period in Selling: A Time to Keep Busy

In all areas of selling there are naturally going to be *slack* periods when you will not be able to actually call on your prospects or conduct sales efforts. During these slow times, the smart salesman will keep active. He will realize that there is never any time to be wasted.

The ambitious retail salesman, for example, will perhaps spend his non-selling time cleaning up the counter. He may inspect the condition of his merchandise, straighten the displays, or rearrange merchandise so that it will have more sales appeal to the next customer who comes in. Many retail salesmen also use this "extra" time to write up orders, make "prospecting" telephone calls, wrap packages, and so on. In other words, there is absolutely no time to "kill." There are always productive chores that need to be done—or even personal needs that can be taken care of during slow times so that they won't interfere with productive times. The really alert and aggressive salesman, for example, may schedule his meals for slack periods—regardless of how apparently inconvenient or unconventional those times may be as mealtimes. Slack hours may also be used for research, good will efforts, and any other necessary leg-work which must be done eventually.

Many top retail executives, department heads and store proprietors select their slowest seasons to visit buying centers. The jeweler will plan his vacation during the slow summer months. The insurance salesman will travel during the Christmas holidays. And, since the Christmas season is the toughest time of year to call on retailers, many aggressive salesmen will do some "selling on the floor" for their larger accounts. The goodwill that they create by lending a helping hand to a good customer who is in desperate need of a professional salesman during his most busy time of year will often mean many extra orders during the year. Naturally, this is extra work with no immediate financial return, and being at home watching television is a much more tempting way to spend these slack periods. However, this type of extra effort means extra dollars. And it also means the difference between a pro and a semi-pro in selling.

Keeping a Diary

Keeping a diary is a very good way to double-check the organization of your time. Naturally, you are usually aware of what you've been doing each day— but, just the same, *record it daily*. Keep a complete time log. It may be a nuisance at first, but it takes only a few minutes to jot down your whereabouts at the end of each hour, or to write down your appointments at the time you make them. After you've kept accurate records for at least a month, you'll be surprised at the valuable information that you can get from your diary. If you are not properly organized, it will definitely show up in your record. You'll begin to see whether you're using your time wisely—whether you're starting your work-day early enough, spending too much time at lunch, wasting time on unnecessary errands, "visiting" too much with customers, and so on. If you keep honest records, conscientiously, on a daily basis, you'll be able to answer all of these questions and many more. But—a word of caution: *Don't cheat! Put down the gospel truth.* If you "pad" your time log, then you'll only be fooling yourself. It is for *your* sole benefit that you need to keep exact records. *You* are the one who can learn from your mistakes as they appear in black and white.

A Checklist of Important "Time" Tips to Remember

1. *Make Every Call Count.* Don't waste your valuable time on calls that have low potential. Qualify your prospects as best you can *before* investing too much time in personal sales presentations. Try to determine:
   (a) if they actually have a need for your product;
   (b) if they can afford to buy; and
   (c) if they are acceptable credit risks.

of time is surrendered merely to the chance of incidents, all things lie huddled together in one chaos."

Author Unknown

IX

KNOWING THE TERRITORY

"But he doesn't know the territory!"

"Next stop, River City . . ."

Perhaps in the days of Professor Harold Hill in Meredith Wilson's *The Music Man*, a top-notch salesman could get by without "knowing the territory." But in the highly competitive business world of today, this can't be so. There is much to know about any particular territory, and there can be vast differences between territories. As a professional salesman, you must study your territory . . . you must know as much about it as possible . . . about its geography, its economy, its culture, the makeup of its population, and any other factors that may help you develop better competitive strategies.

How Territories Can Differ

There are thousands of ways in which one territory can differ from others. In this chapter, we will discuss just a few of the more obvious ones . . . the ones that can have the greatest influence on your selling efforts. Naturally, these variables will hold greater or lesser importance to you according to the type of selling you do . . . whether retail, wholesale or industrial . . . and according to the types of products or services that you sell.

One of the obvious—and very important—variables is *climate.* Consider, for example, how weather and seasonal changes affect the business lives of clothing salesmen. Styles and types of fabrics used in clothing will vary greatly between major climatic regions of the country. The sporting-goods salesman, the heating and air-conditioning salesman, and the lawn and garden care salesman are also obviously affected by climate—and there are many others, such as those in automobile sales, home maintenance and repairs, and even such lines as books and magazines. (Think for a moment about how much more reading time people have in the long winter evenings in Minnesota or Michigan, as opposed to people living in Arizona, Florida, or Southern California.)

Another important variable is the *economy* of a region or territory. Income per capita and income per family will fluctuate considerably from one section of the country to another. This greatly affects the sales of many luxury items such as jewelry, furs, color television, and so on. Rolls Royces, obviously, will not be popular in depressed areas such as Southern Kentucky, but their sales potential is quite another matter in more affluent areas such as Miami Beach, Florida. Where incomes are high, it is natural that people will buy more of the "non-necessity" types of goods and services. In other words, they are able to take care of their basic needs, and still have "discretionary" spending power left over for the luxuries. In the lower income areas, however, the salesman will find himself competing for a share of much more limited spending power.

Other economic factors, such as labor unions (which can cripple an area with strikes) can also make a tremendous difference to a territory. Cities and towns that depend on one major industry are more vulnerable to economic ups-and-downs than are the highly-diversified communities. Local politics can have a strong effect on the economy of an area. And, naturally, local and state taxes are also important factors. A word of caution, however: Too many salesmen are anxious to excuse their poor record and blame their low production on the economic conditions of their territories, when in many instances this is *not* the problem.

The *culture* and *customs* in different parts of the country also influence the sales of different products. An excellent example is trying to sell life insurance to the Pennsylvania Dutch. It is their custom that the entire community should provide for the grieved widow—so, naturally, their communities are not good places to sell life insurance and estate planning services. Early American furniture will be in more demand in Virginia, for example, than in California. Likewise, clothing fashions in New York City will vastly differ from the midwestern states—and styles in rural areas will differ from styles in metropolitan areas. A traveling salesman in New England might find his prospects more cautious than the friendly Midwesterner, especially if the salesman is a stranger. In other words, the way of life in America greatly differs from coast to coast and casts its influence on peoples' buying habits accordingly.

There are many more factors to consider in weighing the advantages and disadvantages which fluctuate according to the territory. Here are a few examples:

The sale of hunting and fishing supplies will be far better in areas with plenty of forests and streams than in areas where there is little opportunity for outdoor life.

The sale of boating supplies will be more popular in Minnesota (with her 10,000 lakes) than in Kansas or Iowa.

Naturally, heavy farm equipment salesmen will enjoy greater success in the Midwest (the corn belt) than in Rhode Island or Massachusetts.

The "Ivy League" clothing salesman will find a better market and greater demand around Boston than in San Antonio.

The travel agent will enjoy a more enthusiastic market for his European travel tours in sophisticated New York City than he will in the Dakotas.

The office machine salesman will find a greater demand for his products in the larger metropolitan areas.

The industrial salesman in the Cleveland-Akron area will have a far better market than his opposite number in Mississippi or Montana.

Snow-moving equipment will sell better in Maine or

North Dakota than in Arizona—and the same would apply to snowtires, snowchains, anti-freeze, batteries, etc.

Outdoor bar-b-que grills and porch furniture will sell better in Florida or California than in Michigan or Vermont.

Car manufacturers ship more convertibles per capita to Forida and California than to Pennsylvania or Michigan; and more air-conditioned cars are sold in Florida than in Pennsylvania.

There are thousands of other examples that could be added to the list. Use your imagination and discover how your product will be affected by different territories.

Selling Abroad

In today's world, our planet seems to be getting smaller and smaller. Big business and increased competition dictate that salesmen must go after foreign markets more and more every year. It is natural to assume that the international salesman must understand this new complex market if he is to succeed. Since customs, laws, politics, traditions, styles and languages vary so greatly throughout the world, it is very important that the *international salesman* be knowledgeable about the customs of each country in which he does business. The style and pace of business in many countries is the exact opposite of what it is in the United States. Therefore, it's important that the professional salesman *prepare himself* for doing business with his international clients. Here are a few points to be concerned about:

1. Know their language and customs.
2. Learn their taboos.
3. Be sincere . . . do not patronize.
4. Avoid discussing politics.
5. Avoid being too aggressive in countries where the style of doing business is more calm and structured than it is in our country.
6. When dining with a customer, don't criticize his country's food.
7. Don't overtip, and don't be boisterous. Mind your manners.
8. Let them "set the pace." (Naturally, use discretion here.)
9. Learn as much as possible about the other country's history, social patterns, political views towards America, and—naturally—*our* views on the other country.

Be a good will ambassador for the U.S.A. And, above all, *be proud that you are an American.*

Seeking Information About the Territory

When you are assigned to a new area, you should find out *facts* about your new territory as quickly as possible. Rather than finding out the hard way—by trial and error—you may save a lot of unnecessary leg-work by following a few tips:

Talk to Other Salesmen: To get first-hand information about the general acceptance of your product, if there has been another company salesman represented in the territory, it is wise to compare notes with him. If he is sincere, he can offer many tips that will be of great benefit to you. If you are replacing him because he has done a poor job, be careful not to be swayed by any negative attitude he may display. If the man you are replacing has been "moved upstairs," he should be the best source of information. If possible, it is also helpful to talk to salesmen in related fields. In the majority of cases, these men are eager to be of assistance to a new man in the territory.

Visit the Chamber of Commerce and Better Business Bureau: These two organizations (both state and local) can offer a wealth of information to the newcomer. They are especially helpful in offering information on such things as the historical background of the area, its economic trends, tax information, population trends, natural resources of the area, recreation facilities, climate conditions, and so on. Don't hesitate to use their services. This is what they exist for. It is also good business to *join* the chamber of commerce and the Better Business Bureau.

Talk to Old Customers: If you are going to work a territory in which your company has already been represented, it is advisable to visit with *old* customers. Not only will you want to see them for reorders, but also a visit may offer a fine way to start a conversation and thereby get to know them. Many times, they may put you in touch with other prospects.

Do Research: The *libraries* are full of books that will offer valuable information about your territory. There is practically nothing that cannot be found through smart researching at the local libraries.

Read the Local Newspapers: The local newspapers are excellent sources of information about your territory. A close study of a community's newspaper will help you understand many facets of your new territory— including its cultural and social customs, politics, economy, taxes, business structure, and future growth prospects.

Conclusion

Be careful that you are not swayed by inaccurate information about a new area. All of the sources mentioned in this chapter are valuable information sources, but you should also be careful and analytical about what you read, see and hear. Beware of jumping to conclusions from biased opinions. After all, as a professional salesman, *you* are largely the master of your own fate. You make your own decisions—and you certainly want to make those decisions on the basis of accurate and relevant information. In other words, you want to *know the territory!*

X

SIZING UP YOUR PROSPECT

Sizing up your prospect is like walking on eggs: You have to tread lightly. The professional salesman must know as much as possible about his prospect. The more information he has, the better his chances are for success.

Again, selling is based on the law of averages—and the more the salesman knows about his prospect, the better his odds will be. Sizing up a prospect is a "sixth sense" which all good salesmen develop. This sense—or instinct—makes the professional salesman super-sensitive to each change of mood or attitude on the part of his prospect. It enables him to create a comfortable sales atmosphere; it helps him chart his prospect's mind: and it enables him to ask questions carefully to get the answers he wants.

There are many questions that the professional salesman will ask himself—and answer—before approaching his prospect: Should I spend the time calling on this prospect? Can he afford to buy? Is he sincerely interested? Can he take action *now*? Is a call-back worthwhile? Is now the right time to close the sale?

Every salesman must be able to come up with the right answers to these questions before and during each sales effort.

A word of caution: It is very important that you do not confuse "sizing up" with "prejudging" a prospect. When you size up a customer, you are making a survey of his needs and personality. Do not make the mistake of *prejudging* him. Too often the non-professional salesman will prejudge his prospect by thinking: *"He probably can't afford to buy my product. I think I'll pass him up and call on somebody else!"* A professional salesman will not jump to such fast conclusions. He has learned through experience that many of the prospects who originally "could not afford" to buy have become his finest customers!

Prospecting . . . Who Is a Prospect?

All salesmen realize the importance of prospecting—but few have the ability to make a proper evaluation. They lack the talent to size up a prospect. It is a safe assumption that a salesman cannot call on everybody if he values his time. Thus, the talent of choosing the right prospects must be developed early in the game. Developing the talent of "educated guessing" will certainly go a long way in making your odds more favorable. Naturally, there is no sure-fire way of developing a 100 percent method of "weeding out the bad" —but certain tactics greatly increase your "law of averages" in selling. No matter what product you sell, there is a sound system which you can develop to size up your prospect and save you valuable time in the field.

If your selling involves giving exclusiveness to a dealer, the problem of sizing up a prospect is relatively simple. It is *no* problem whatsoever to find out who the best dealer in town is. Certainly, you should be sure, and you should check for things like: credit rating, volume of store's sales, advertising, and the reputation of the store. This information is simple enough to get, but it becomes more difficult when you must choose a second or third store in the event that the top dealer cannot handle your line.

How do you determine *"who* is actually a prospect?" the answer, again, is relatively simple: It all depends on what you are selling. If you are opening up new accounts with a furniture line, it becomes a simple choice of finding the store that can do your company the most justice within your price range. If your line is men's clothing, for example, you must find a store that caters to your style of clothing in terms of *price, age* and *fashion.* Much of this information can be gleaned from such sources as other salesmen, advertisements (comparing other lines in ads which compliment yours), location of store, friends who live in the community, and the reputation of the store.

The photostatic copying equipment salesman, for

example, certainly must learn to decide who his prospects are. If not, he will surely waste the majority of his time making calls on all businesses at random. After a careful survey of his territory, however, he would more than likely conclude that the following would be good prospects in his area to call on: *insurance agencies, law firms, realtors,* different *sales organizations* in the area, *banks,* medium-size *restaurants* who change their menus daily, and various other *retailers* and *professional people* who send out a lot of billing. He certainly would not waste his time calling on such businesses as small gas stations or auto body garages, because he realizes they would have very little need for his product.

If you are in *direct* selling, it is sometimes harder to size up your prospect. Everybody may be a prospect for the insurance agent—but, naturally, the insurance agent cannot call on everybody right out of the telephone book. He must "prospect" a certain market in terms of: *income, size of family, occupation, age groups, sex* —and sometimes even *religion* (certain religions, for example, do not believe in insurance). The educational salesman, for example, will look for prospects who qualify within a certain age group (preferably just out of high school). The baby-photo salesman will size up his prospects according to the ages of their children! The office equipment salesman will keep a sharp lookout for new businesses and branch offices opening in his territory. The automobile salesman will size up his prospects according to the year, model, and condition of the cars they are driving.

The real estate salesman selling homes will look for such clues as: prospects who are now renting, size of the families, estimated income, ages of children (which determine the possible importance of living near a school), religion (which will be a factor if a church is nearby) . . . and so on. It is obvious that every product sold will have individual factors which must be carefully weighed and appraised to properly size up *who is a prospect* in a given field.

Once everything else is determined, it is important to consider your prospect's *ability to pay*. Naturally, it is quite useless to sell a man on the need of your product and then learn that his credit is bad. It puts no commission in your pocket to sell an account and then have your company turn it down because of poor credit! It is not always possible to know this information before calling on a prospect—but, whenever reliable information can be obtained, it is wise to get it beforehand!

Dun & Bradstreet is one of several credit rating sources to check credit and ability to pay. Listen carefully to the comments of other salesmen and other customers—but learn not to believe everything you hear. Naturally, rumors should be discounted, but you should learn to pay close attention to the source. Signs of prosperity—such as a new car, a fancy home, expensive vacations, country club memberships, a new boat, etc.—can give good clues, but they can also be very misleading!

It would be foolish to say that you can size up every prospect and "guess" correctly! Every department store sales-person has been warned of the individual who dresses like a pauper, but who can "buy out the store." On the other hand, there is the four-flusher who can't afford to buy a cup of coffee, but who dresses expensively. It is important to know how to recognize the "exception to the rule." Of course, in the long run, the exception to the rule won't greatly alter your success! The important rule to remember in sizing up your prospect is: Learn to value your time and avoid wasting it on poor prospects. "Time is money."

The Timing Element in Prospecting

Undoubtedly, you have often heard the cliché; "being at the right place at the right time." And, there is no doubt about it—this wise saying makes a lot of sense. In sizing up a prospect before you are ready to make the actual call, it is important to consider the timing element. If you choose the *wrong* time to see your prospect, it can very easily cost you a sale. Some of the wrong times may be:

> *When the Prospect Is in a Hurry.* If you try to pin down a man who is just putting on his coat and is ready to step out the door, you are wasting an otherwise good prospect. Never present your product to a person under these circumstances, because you cannot possibly get the attention you need. In cases like this, simply make a definite appointment for another date that will be convenient to both of you.
>
> *The Worried Prospect.* Sometimes there are prospects who may be unusually worried about a problem just at

the time when you contact them to make a sales presentation. Perhaps there has been an accident, a death in the family, a fire, or business has been terrible, and so on. If you sense that your prospect is under unusual strain, it is better that you do not talk to him at that time. He simply will not be able to concentrate on your presentation—nor is he likely to be in a position or frame of mind to make a decision. Again, you should set up another date to see him.

The Tired Prospect. If your selling is done in the evening (educational sales, insurance, home improvements, etc.) and you find a prospect who can hardly keep his eyes open, it is senseless to talk to him. He won't be capable of listening to you. Don't forget: Some prospects get up several hours before you do (for example, farmers, construction workers, bakers, post office employees, service station operators, etc.) *and they go to bed several hours before you do.* A man who is about to fall asleep cannot give you his undivided attention any more than the hurried man can. In cases such as this, it is necessary to arrange an interview immediately following dinner or on a day-off or a weekend.

The Preoccupied Prospect. It is just plain good sense not to interrupt a prospect while he is preoccupied with something else. Of course, most people will stop work to listen to your sales presentation—if only out of courtesy—but at times it will hurt your chances of success. Often a man will stop working on a machine, or climb down from a roof-top to listen to a salesman, but his mind will be preoccupied with what he was doing. Many sales have been made under conditions where, for example, a prospect has climbed down from his tractor in the field, stopped milking his cow, left his lawn mower running, pulled his truck over to the side of the road, turned off his TV during a World Series, or even walked away from his own customer! But working under such conditions—where you interrupt your prospect—is generally *not* to your advantage. See your prospect at times when you will be able to receive his full attention, and you will be playing with better odds!

As you can see, timing can play an important role in determining the outcome of your sales presentation. Learn to size up the favorable time conditions of your prospect, and *your percentages* will be more favorable. Always remember: Under more favorable conditions, the man who said "no" might have said "yes!"

Sizing Up Different Types of Buyers

Human behavior patterns and buying patterns naturally vary among different types of people. In order to be a successful salesman, you must be able to size up your customer's buying patterns and gauge what type of person he is. How you handle your buyer will vary from customer to customer, depending upon how you *size him up*. Here are a few of the basic types of customers you will most likely come across:

The Uncommunicative or Silent Customer. This type of person is a real puzzle to many salesmen. He is not only silent, but he also often has a scowl or frown which tends to unnerve some salesmen. Treat this type of person with *courtesy;* be very pleasant; smile often; and give him reassurance to win his confidence. Explain your product very carefully and stress its quality. Once you sell this type of individual, you have made a conquest and a life-long customer. Don't talk too fast with him, but be enthusiastic.

The Impulse Buyer. This type is a "man of action"—

a fast thinker. He is restless and quick to make decisions. Don't waste time explaining small details unless he asks for them. Don't oversell or try to build a castle in the sky. Try to avoid flowery words and sentences, since you are interested in keeping his attention and you don't want his mind to drift.

The Deliberate or Meditative Buyer. This type of buyer is just the opposite of the impulse buyer. He is slower-moving and wants to know the small details. He is very careful and methodical in making a decision. It is important that he understand everything throughly—so be sure to give him complete answers to any questions he asks. Make sure that he understands everything you say, and constantly ask him: "Are there any questions so far?" Paint vivid word pictures. Take your time with this buyer, and be ready to spend a long time with him.

The Buddy-Buddy Buyer. This person is very friendly and easy to talk to, but can be very tough to sell. He has a built-in resistance towards salesmen and he tries to change the subject and draw you off-track so he will not have to buy. Don't allow this friendly character to overcome you with charm. Don't get out-maneuvered. Don't drift away from your sales presentation. If you use his friendliness and charm to *your* advantage in a subtle manner, you can control the sales interview.

The Egotistical Customer. This type of customer is very confident. He usually has a great deal of vanity and he constantly tries to impress everybody with his knowledge. Never argue a point with him—even when he is wrong. If you do, you will injure his pride and lose the sale. It may even be necessary to flatter him at times and allow him to believe he is an expert. Let him make decisions, and compliment him for his ability to pass judgment so quickly. It is important never to criticize this type of individual—not even if he asks your opinion or invites criticism. Be very diplomatic. If he asks for your views, give them as *suggestions,* and ask what he thinks about them. Keep building up his ego, and you will be able to do business with him.

The Hesitant or Undecided Buyer. As we discussed earlier, many people are afraid to make decisions. You must win this type of individual's confidence and make it *easy* for him to buy. Give him many *minor* decisions to make, such as: "Do you want to have this shipped by truck or rail?" "Do you prefer the green or blue model?" "Do you prefer to pay by check or cash?" Never give him too large a decision to make.

During the Sales Interview

There is quite a bit of "sizing up" to be done during the actual sales interview. Naturally, all buyers are different—and each must be handled somewhat differently than the other. The professional salesman recognizes this and acts accordingly. He is able to form definite opinions of the buyer (from his reactions) and guide the sales interview to best fit the situation. Ed Ellman* says, "BE A GOOD LISTENER. The hardest part of selling or communicating is listening. Create a climate for your prospect to talk about his achievements, his disappointments, his concerns. This will tell you where his greatest insurance needs are. After you have listened very carefully, you can show him with insurance dollars how his efforts will be guaranteed in the future." In this manner, even the professional salesman with the so-called "canned" presentation can custom-make his sales interview to fit

*Edwin M. Ellman—Senior principal of Edwin M. Ellman & Associates, one of the nation's largest life isurance brokers, President of Ellman Financial & Service Corporation and principal in an investment funding firm, Capital Acquisition & Investment Corp.

each prospect. Here are a few examples of cases where a professional salesman will do this:

Rational or Emotional Approach? The professional salesman may ask himself which approach—*rational* or emotional—would be best for his customer.

1. A good life insurance agent, for example, may figure: "I would be wiser to appeal to this man's love for his family, rather than sell him on a tax advantage appeal."

2. The experienced automobile salesman may size up his prospect and think to himself: "This man should be sold on the economy of the car, rather than the value of owning the car as a status symbol."

3. The clothing salesman may size up his prospect by thinking: "He definitely seems to be the man who wants a suit to last for a long time, rather than a man who is interested in styles."

4. The real estate man may size up his prospect by thinking: "These people are definitely more interested in a fancy address, rather than the construction of the house." (He then proceeds to impress them with the important people who live in the neighborhood.)

Is the Buyer Sincerely Interested? This a question which every professional salesman asks himself during a sales interview. After the sales presentation has been in progress for a certain period of time, it is important to determine whether or not your prospect "feels the need" for your product. It is obviously useless to give a long, drawn out presentation if you are certain that your prospect has no interest in your product. Learn to "size up" your prospect at a given place in your sales interview, and form definite opinions as to whether or not it is useful to proceed any further. There are key questions which you may ask to help determine this for you. For example—

1. The career health and accident insurance agent has learned to "feel out" his prospect by asking questions such as: "Mr. Jones, can you and your family use a guaranteed monthly income each month, such as this program will provide, whenever you are sick or hurt and unable to work?" (The ball is now handed to the prospect, and he must give a clue as to his actual interest.)

2. The automobile salesman sizes up his prospect with the question: "Are you planning to drive this beauty out today, Mr. Smith?"

3. The salesman selling fountain pens will allow his prospect to write a few lines, and then he sizes him up with a leading question: "Isn't this the best fountain pen for the money on the market?"

4. The successful shoe salesman will size up his customer by letting him first walk around in the best pair, and then ask: "Don't you agree, Mr. Brown, your feet have never felt so comfortable?" There is little time to be spent on the prospect who is merely "shopping around" and has no intention of buying. The leading questions we have suggested above can pretty well *size up* this type of individual. Naturally, this kind of sizing up must be done with real finesse, so that you will not offend your buyer with questions that are too obvious.

Is It Now Time to Close? At different intervals in your sales presentation, it will naturally be time to close the sale. Careful sizing up of your buyer must be done to determine *when!* If you do not recognize this time when he is ready to buy, you are risking the possibility of overselling, and you can literally talk yourself out of a sale! On the other hand, there is the stubborn buyer who needs more convincing before he will reach a decision to buy. Or, perhaps you may encounter the cautious buyer who will not make a decision until you have given all the facts in great detail. Each buyer must be sized up properly before you, the salesman, can know exactly where and how to close the sale. There is little room for guesswork in the close. As we will discuss in detail in a later chapter, the closing of a sale is a technique which must be mastered with professionalism.

Callbacks. All salesmen must determine whether or not it is advisable to spend the additional time to see the prospect at a later date for a decision to buy or not. Naturally, in some fields of selling this must be done all the time—but in others the "callback" may be a complete waste of time and effort. Each salesman must devop the ability to size up his prospect and realize the value (or disadvantage) in making a callback. Ask yourself the question: "Is it worthwhile to call back again on Mr. Prospect, or would it be wiser to go 'double-or-nothing' and either get the sale today or never?" Learn the cold hard facts of selling—that the average buyer would rather give you a "maybe" for tomorrow rather than say "yes" today! Also realize that the "law of diminishing returns" is very relevant in selling: The prospect will have the strongest desire for the product *immediately after it has been presented to him.* The longer the period of time that lapses between now and actually making a decision to buy, the more he will value his money and the less he will desire the product. He will cool off! With this in mind, it is very important that you plan your callbacks *only after you have correctly sized up your prospects.*

Conclusion

In a nutshell, sizing up your prospect helps you play the percentages a little better. It is a very definite factor in determining your chances of success with any prospect. It's the talent of *thinking on your own two feet* while under the pressure of the "big guns." It is a talent which, as has just been illustrated, must be used in *all phases of selling.* Develop this talent for sizing up your prospect, and your sales production will soar!

XI

"BEING IMPORTANT" IS *VERY* IMPORTANT

If you want to be highly successful in selling, it is essential that you generate "an air of importance" when calling on prospects. Your prospect must think: "Here is an *important person* . . . I must listen to what he has to offer. I know it will be *important!*"

Unless your prospect is in this frame of mind, the task of selling him will be completely uphill—and you will be fighting against heavy odds.

With the fast pace of living in today's business world, it is virtually impossible for a businessman to spend time with all the salesmen who call on him and listen to their sales presentations. If he did, his business would certainly be neglected. At the same time, however, he also realizes that the progress of his business is dependent to a certain extent on the important information which he receives from salesmen. With this thought in mind, we can safely state that the typi-

cal businessman must "weed out" certain salesmen—
he must choose the ones he will see, and the ones he
will not see. This, of course, applies to *all* buyers—not
just executives and proprietors. At any rate, it is obvious how much more receptive the typical executive or
buyer will be toward the salesmen who appear to him
to be important. After all, *his time* is important to him
—and he wants to occupy that time only with important matters and important people.

The salesman who walks in with *importance* radiat-
ing all over him will nearly always get the sales interview. His prospect will think: "Here is a man who
counts for something. I'll surely benefit by listening to
this man. He's bound to have something useful to
say."

On the other hand, the run-of-the-mill salesman
will give an impression that says: "Oh no, another
salesman! I can't listen to him . . . I am far too busy.
If I listened to every salesman who called on me, I
would be broke by now. I'll give him a quick brush-
off." In this case, it's not that the prospect is necessarily trying to be rude—but he realizes that he can
allocate only part of his time to salesmen—and this
salesman doesn't warrant the time.

Analyzing "Being Important"

Like everybody else, you probably have many
salesmen who call on you at your office, store or home.
Think for a few minutes, and then ask yourself: "Why
do I listen to *some* salesmen and yet flatly refuse to

listen to *others*? It doesn't really make much difference what company they represent—or what product they sell. It's the *salesman* who really makes the difference! When I do give an audience to a salesman, *what* is it that makes me give him such *preferred treatment*?"

Chances are, you can't really answer this question. But, somehow, the salesman impressed you that he is *important*. It's that simple! Everybody is interested in what an *important person* has to say—but the unimportant man is ignored.

In sales, it's the *salesman* who creates the "executive image" people want to associate with. It's the man who walks in "like he belongs there" who commands respect.

For example, if a salesman who looked and acted exactly like Gregory Peck (or George Romney, Johnny Carson, Ronald Reagan—take your pick) were to call on you, what would your reaction be? It wouldn't make a bit of difference what company he represented. He could be selling pencils, magazines or pots and pans; it wouldn't matter. It's the *important image* which he creates that would make you want to listen to him. It's the *man* that we are attracted to. The salesman who has a distinguished appearance, a supremely confident appearance, a dynamic appearance or an aggressive appearance will create an excitement that demands immediate attention and response.

On the other hand, think about the times you ignored salesmen for no apparent reason other than "you were simply not interested." Not interested in *what*? Chances are you didn't even know . . . or care!

It's a cruel world, perhaps, but nobody has time to listen to the down-and-outer. *The salesman who represents failure is simply not worthy of being listened to.* After all, what does *he* know? How can anybody benefit from a failure? Unimportant people are uninteresting. Unsuccessful men are depressing to be around.

But remember: *People are attracted to successful people.* (How many times have we heard that "success breeds success?")

Don't Overlook the Secretary

The impression you leave with your prospect's secretary is extremely important.

What does she say to her boss when she hands him your business card? Does she say, "Mr. Smith is here to see you, and it seems very important that he talk with you now?" Or perhaps she says, "There's another salesman out in the reception room—a Mr. what's-his-name. Shall I tell him you're too busy to see him?"

The proprietor, executive, department head, and buyer are not the only people you must impress. As a matter of fact, you may not even get the chance to work your charisma on them unless you are able to work it first on the people who often do the "screening"—the secretary, the receptionist, or the "gal Friday."

As you can see, *creating an important image with the girl out front can make a big difference!*

"Being Important" Conserves Your Time

If your prospect believes that you are important, he will naturally show more respect for your time. Notice how this works the next time you're in a reception room waiting to see a buyer. Look around at the other salesmen. You can bet the ones who have been waiting the longest are probably the least successful. The important ones aren't kept waiting; they are shown right in—usually ahead of their turns. It may seem unfair, but it happens every day.

"Being Important" and Your Sales Presentation

Not only will "being important" create a better first impression—which will give you the chance to present your product—but also it will make your entire sales presentation run more smoothly. You will discover how much more attentively your prospect listens to you. He will take what you have to say more seriously and will not want to miss anything important. He will think of you as an "expert."

Every salesman realizes how disturbing an interruption can be—especially at a crucial moment during a sales interview. But, barring an unexpected emergency, your buyer will not dare interrupt you if he is sufficiently impressed that you are *"important!"* On the other hand, the buyer is apt to be carrying on all sorts of other business while the *un*impressive, *un*important salesman is attempting to make a presentation. Not only will he *take* telephone calls, but also he is not apt to concern himself with *how much time* he talks on the phone. He may even off-handedly sign letters, riffle through his in-coming mail, or bend paper-clips into sculptured shapes—while the hapless salesman drones on with a rote presentation that is doomed to utter failure.

There are even further benefits that the "important" salesman can enjoy. For example, when a salesman acts important, his buyer is not likely to interrupt him with untimely questions during a sales interview. The buyer will respect the salesman's judgment and will anticipate that all of his key questions will be answered in due time during the presentation. What's more, if a prospect respects the salesman as an important person, he will not burden that salesman with the inconvenience of calling back on him after he "thinks over" the offer. He won't give the salesman a "run-around." Instead, he is more apt to give him a positive answer *today*. In other words, most people simply don't impose on other people whom they consider important.

Your Service Is Important

Sure, you act important and you look important. But always remember: YOU ARE IMPORTANT. You are performing a vital service for your client. Ed Ellman says, "A successful life insurance agent conveys importance by understanding his prospect's problem or opportunities, either by research before calling or listening effectively during the interview and communicating dramatically that understanding. After you have sized up the problem, you add, 'Mr. Prospect, I know how much time you devote to create the cash you need to make this business run. Let me show you how you can create more capital now, strengthen your business and either lift a heavy burden from your family or make it possible for them to continue. Through your sound planning this enterprise which you are developing will enable your family to continue running the business in the event of your death without draining the capital.' "

As you can see from the above illustration of Mr. Ellman's, the professional salesman can, as an advisor, perform a very important service to his client, which will solve otherwise "unsolved problems."

Conclusion

"Being important" is really what professional selling is all about. Not only will it get you many more interviews, but it will make for smoother sailing once you have begun a sales interview. Furthermore, it will make a big difference in your closing rate—which is so important for high productivity.

Perhaps now it would be useful for you to reread Chapter VII on "Appearance and Sales Etiquette." Naturally, your appearance and sales etiquette standards will have a direct bearing on the "important image" you generate. All of your mannerisms will directly affect this critical part of your selling approach.

And, by the way—as an extra fringe benefit, you are bound to enjoy your work far more if you carry yourself with an air of importance. Unfortunately, the American public often has a negative attitude toward the salesman—and this leads in many cases to abuse and ridicule. But, you *can* operate in a different "league." With all the other high standards necessary to the *professional* salesman, you can—through the added dimension of "being important"—enjoy both self-respect and the respect of others—as well as success and prosperity.

XII

"REVERSE" IN SELLING

Warning! The information contained in this chapter is not for the amateur. It represents a very effective selling method when used by the highly skilled and experienced professional salesman. But the novice should not try this technique.

If you feel as though you can qualify . . . if you're a true professional salesman . . . then *read on. Reverse selling* is one of *the most* highly advanced techniques in the field of salesmanship. But beware! Unless you are a skilled pro—a big leaguer—don't use this method. It can be disastrous if used by the unskilled . . . and yet, when used with finesse, it can bring amazing results. It can help you make sales that would be lost with any other method.

Reverse selling is a technique which completely disarms your prospect. It provides an unexpected change of pace. It should only be used in a pinch, when all else seems to be destined to fail. It should also be used only by the salesman who is good at *sizing*

128

up his prospect, and by the salesman who has an excellent sense of *timing*. If you misjudge your prospect, or mistime your use of the reverse method, you may anger or offend your would-be customer.

In effect, through the reverse method you are "putting it on the line" to your prospect. You emphasize the fact that he must make a decision if he feels the need for your product. The degree with which you employ this method depends on your basic selling skills. Don't use it until you know what you're doing, and until you have your timing down pat.

The "Independent" Approach

Play it cool. One of the most subtle ways of using the reverse technique is to act relaxed and casual, assuming an attitude that your product is very special . . . that you are doing the buyer a service by calling on him. But *don't overdo* this attitude. Don't overplay the part. In this day and age, the buyer feels that it is *his* prerogative, and not the salesman's, to act aloof. When you, the salesman, act in this manner you are completely "reversing" your buyer's position or relationship to you. While the mediocre salesman bows down to his buyer's every wish and command, the professional salesman *reverses the situation* and elevates himself in relation to the buyer. To the amateur, this may sound impossible—especially in the highly competitive markets we have today—but professional salesmen are using this method daily . . . and it's highly effective!

One way of easing into a reverse posture would go something like this: "Please understand this, Mr. Prospect. Our company only has a *limited* supply of this special material available. Our capacity is limited in this particular range in the number of suits we can manufacture. Since you've been a regular customer of ours for years, I'm going to allocate an extra dozen suits over and above your present order."

This technique of selling was common during World War II when goods were extremely scarce, but *good* salesmen still employ similar tactics. The limited offer technique is used daily. For example, how many times have you gone into the grocery store and been told, "Only one to a customer?" This independent attitude makes the buyer want the product because the seller is really saying, "This is such an excellent value, I must limit my offer so that all my good customers can be rewarded for their loyalty." The seller is limiting the offer because he is absolutely confident that he will sell out completely. What independence! What *reverse!*

Offering "exclusiveness in reputation" is another form of reverse selling. The "independent" salesman says, "Our firm only allows the finest dress shops in the country to handle our line. We have a reputation to live up to and wouldn't want a run-of-the-mill store to ruin our name. It's our opinion that your firm is worthy of our product." This is *powerful* selling.

Offering a dealer exclusiveness in handling your product in his territory can also be reverse selling. Be independent, and say, "Look, Mr. Dealer, we are only going to permit one outlet in this town to handle our

line. If you are not able to order a large enough quantity of our goods, I'm afraid I'll be forced to take the line away from you and give it to your competition down the street who wants it very badly. I know you don't want to lose your following, which our company has helped you establish with our good name, so let's increase this order to give you a representative selection, and at the same time, increase your profits."

If you use this method of reverse selling effectively, your sales will soar. But, *a word of caution:* If you use it improperly (or on the wrong buyer) you can imagine what he will tell you to do with your line!

The straight-commission salesman can also act independent, as though he were paid on salary, and say, "Look, Mr. Prospect, I am on salary, so frankly it doesn't make a bit of difference to me personally what you do. But let me caution you. This is the last one we have in stock at this price. After the first of the month, the price will go up—providing we even get more of these in. It won't make me any richer or poorer, no matter what you do—but my advice is, grab it now while you can."

The "independence" of the salaried salesman . . . the attitude that he does not personally profit . . . will sway many prospects. It throws the prospect off guard because the salesman does not appear to be using any pressure. Sure, this may sound like high pressure, but it works on certain prospects who like to sit on the fence. Again, you can't use it on everybody . . . and you have to be convincing when you do use it! Ordinarily, it's a last ditch effort.

Playing "Hard to Get"

Do you remember, when you were young, how much you were in love with the pretty little blonde— *until you actually won her heart?* The minute she stopped playing hard to get, your "love" for her vanished. It is human nature to want things that are hard to get. This little lesson plays an important role in reverse selling. After all, why would people spend small fortunes on diamonds if they were not hard to get?

Having a prospect believe he may not be able to purchase your product will make him want it all the more. For example, in selling insurance, a good way to reverse the prospect might go something like this: "Mr. Prospect, your application looks questionable to me. I have my reservations about your qualifying, but let's leave that up to the doctor who gives you the exam." It's a well known fact that the person who has poor health . . . who may not be insurable . . . will take all the insurance he can afford and all he can *get!* Not that he believes he needs it more than the healthy person, but he wants it "because he can get it."

Herbert L. Greenberg, one of the nation's leading insurance sales authorities, always used reverse selling when closing a sale by saying, "If you knew that this would be the last opportunity that you would ever have to obtain life insurance, would you take advantage of it?" After a long pause, Herb would add, "All the money in the world won't buy you insurability once you have lost your health!" Herb claims that many of his clients took out additional amounts of insurance with this simple added thought provoker.

Another good example of the power of exclusiveness and scarcity is the *country club*. Country clubs would not exist today if they didn't sell *exclusiveness*. In fact, many people join a certain country club because it is known to be the *hardest* to get into!

If you use this same kind of psychology in your selling, it can be a *powerful tool.* Here's the way it can work: "Mr. Buyer, in order for your department store to have the exclusive on our line in this city, I must have a bigger order than this one. My company will tear it up if I dare send in such a small order. If you want to qualify as our store in this city, let's increase this order by twenty dozen." Then, the salesman might add, "It could be that the home office will not want to do business with this store, no matter what size the order. As you know, our firm only deals with the prestige store in each major city. I frankly don't know whether they will feel this is *the right store!*" The buyer's reaction, hopefully, would be: "Actually I believe we can do the best job in town. We are *the* store! Let's make that thirty dozen!"

By making the product hard to get, the salesman has reversed his buyer into wanting to be "acceptable."

Here is yet another illustration: The *Continental* (Lincoln, special series, limited number manufactured) was originally sold to only certain "qualified" individuals. In order to qualify, a buyer had to have a certain income. This made the car "hard to get"—and thus created more desire for people to obtain one. The good Continental salesman would cross-examine his prospect with questions concerning his job, his income and his credit. The more questions asked, the more effect the reverse technique had on the prospect. Many people undoubtedly bought Continentals partly just to see if they could "qualify" for one! Great reverse selling!

"Throwing a Challenge"

Another form of reverse selling is "throwing a challenge" to the buyer. Sometimes, throwing the "right curve" at the right time can be very effective in closing a sale. Again, a word of caution: *"Challenging" your prospect must be done properly, or it shouldn't be done at all!*

Take, for example, Mrs. Housekeeper, who has spent the last forty-five minutes in the appliance department shopping for a dryer—and still cannot make up her mind. The salesman, after exhausting all other techniques in trying to close this sale, challenges her with this statement: "Does your husband complain that his back aches from carrying heavy loads back and forth from the basement to the back yard?" With this, she snaps, "What do you mean? *His* back! *I* am the one that does the laundry in our house!" The salesman then smiles and says, "Then, don't you think it's your decision to buy this dryer?" Bingo! A sale is made.

Another situation may involve a purchasing agent

who procrastinates and cannot decide whether he should take action immediately, or wait. Again, reversing the buyer with a challenge may do the trick. The salesman may say, "I must be talking to the wrong man, Mr. Buyer. I was under the impression that you had the authority to make such a decision to buy at this time." The purchasing agent may reply, "Of *course*, I have the authority. And when you bill this order, make sure you mark it to my *personal* attention!" Perhaps a bit risky, but if done properly, this type of selling gets big results.

The life insurance agent challenges his prospect by saying, "Tom, you are the man (bread winner) in the house. Certainly you don't need your wife's permission to make the decision whether or not you should apply for this life insurance program which I have just explained to you! What if she said she didn't want you to have any life insurance? Would that mean that you wouldn't provide life insurance for your widow and beloved children? Of course not! Regardless of what her opinion is, you must have life insurance. You know, Tom, almost all wives complain that their husbands have too much life insurance, but you know something, I never heard a widow complain about it. It's certainly your decision to make, not her's!"

"It may be more than you can afford," challenges the mutual fund salesman. "Seventy-five dollars a month is probably too much of a burden to you at this time." But, his prospect, who has been put on the spot by this remark, may come back with something like this: "Well, I don't know about that. In fact, why don't you put me down for $100 per month!"

Another challenge has been accepted! Another sale has been made!

When dealing with one partner where there is another partner involved, a good challenge to the indecisive buyer may be: "Doesn't your *partner* trust you in making such decisions?" If you say this at the right time, your prospect will probably reply: "Of course, he has confidence in my ability to make decisions! That's why we are partners. Put us down for a large one."

Another challenge may be: "Perhaps this is too big a decision for you to handle?" (This is surely a challenge to a man's pride and his ability to stand on his own two feet.)

Sometimes a procrastinator may be stimulated by this approach: "Without being able to make changes, there would be no progress. You *are* interested in progress, aren't you?"

There are many challenges that will bring additional sales . . . but remember, they must be said to the *right person* and at the *right time*.

Acting Important

Acting important is another form of reversing the prospect. Instead of "polishing apples"—like a typical run-of-the-mill salesman—the *professional* salesman impresses the buyer with how important he is. Too many salesmen are *afraid* of the buyer and are more than willing to take all that he can dish out. Acting as though *you* are the "important" party is excellent reverse selling.

Instead of waiting in a reception room for an hour and a half, the *professional* salesman waits only a few minutes and then tells the receptionist: "You will have to excuse me, but my tight schedule won't permit me to spend any more time waiting."

After this, he sets up a *firm* appointment on another date. The prospect has to respect the salesman for acting like this, and it is a sure bet that the reception will be much warmer on his next visit.

Acting "important" is stressed strongly in top-notch sales organizations, as witnessed by the fancy titles that many such organizations give their salesmen. It is rare when you see a business card with the plain title of "Salesman" on it. Instead, you'll see such titles as: *Vice President, Special Account Executive, District Supervisor, Sales Manager, Field Superintendent,* and so on. These titles are used to *impress* the buyer that he is not dealing with an "ordinary" salesman but with a *professional* . . . with somebody at a higher level.

By impressing the buyer with his importance, the salesman finds himself in a stronger position to influence the sale.

"Acting important" can play a very strong role in professional selling.

Conclusion

If you are a salesman who is just starting a new job, it is very likely that the company you are now

working for used *reverse selling when you recruited you.*
Top organizations that are sales-oriented use reverse
selling during their interviews of prospective salesmen. They make the job "hard to get"—and they use
the "can you qualify?" technique in making the job
sound desirable. These companies realize that a *good*
salesman will not want a position that "just anybody"
can have. So, the harder the job is to get, the better
the salesman they will attract. Again, *excellent reverse
selling!*

If you will reread the introduction tto this chapter, you will see an example of reverse selling. Warning the reader that this chapter was not for the amateur, but only for the *skilled,* experienced, professional
salesman was a *direct challenge* . . . and it probably made
you read it more intently. Each salesman who reads
this chapter wants to "qualify" as a skilled salesman,
rather than an amateur. Undoubtedly, the warning did
not discourage anybody from reading this chapter.
Rather, it *challenged* the alert and serious reader.

It is, however, very important that reverse selling
be mastered before it is to be used. It can be *very
dangerous* if not used properly and intelligently. Think
of different methods of reverse selling you can use in
your field, and practice them *many times* before you try
them. Then, go out and reverse 'em!

It was Groucho Marx who once said: "If this country club is willing to accept *me* as a member, then I
don't want to belong!"

Think about that! Then, think about it some
more, in context with what you've just read on the
subject of *reverse selling.*

XIII

THE ART OF HANDLING REBUTTALS

Every salesman should get used to hearing the word *"no"* because it's almost a natural instinct for a buyer to react negatively until he is *thoroughly convinced* of the advantages of buying a product. When the buyer says *"yes,"* he realizes that it is going to *cost him money*—so, unless he is absolutely sold on the need for a product, he is going to react negatively and *hold onto his money.* Thus, it is very important for you, as a salesman, to realize that a *"no"* does not necessarily mean, "No, I definitely will not buy!" It means, rather, "I am not convinced yet; give me a reason *why* I should buy."

Naturally, there are going to be times when the buyer says "no" and it will be *final*—and there will *not* be a sale. But don't forget that selling is a "law-of-average" business, and you can't sell 'em all. However, it is important to realize that a good percentage of your prospects who say "no" once—or even several times—can still be sold if they are thoroughly convinced of the benefits of buying your product. Show your prospect what it will do for him; make him feel the *need* to own it.

The key rule to remember when you entounter a "no" is: *Objections are merely requests for more information.* The professional salesman does not panic when he is met with these obstacles. He merely uses his reverse of product knowledge and sales know-how and continues with his sales presentation, showing his prospect why he should say *"yes."* It has often been said that *real selling* doesn't actually begin until after the prospect has said "no." Persuading a prospect at this point is what separates the men from the boys.

How to React When the Customer Says "No"

The neophyte salesman might ask: "How do you react when you encounter an objection?" In one word, the answer is: *Calm.* The word "no" is so common to the experienced professional salesman that he doesn't even realize that his customer has spoken negatively! He does, however, hear his customer *ask for additional information,* and he continues to sell the benefits of his product. Learn to RESPECT THE WORD, "NO"— but don't be afraid of it!

Some of the better salesmen are "deaf" to their customer's objections. They don't even hear the word "no." They have a built-in control unit in the back of their heads which drowns out any objections with a loud voice saying "Give me more information. I want to buy from you, but please convince me that I should spend my money wisely on your product."

The weak salesman, on the other hand, will be beaten when he gets an objection. His knees will shake and his tongue will get tied up. His mind will draw a blank, and he is finished! His real fear is based on the premise that the customer has rejected his proposal. He is disappointed because he has been turned down —and he *shows* it! He feels beaten and believes that he has failed. He is ready to pack up his sales gear and move out to another prospect. He has taken the word "no" to mean: "I will not buy *under any circumstances . . . definitely not!*"

Learn to realize the word "no" doesn't really mean denial or refusal. In selling, its definition means: "Give me a reason to buy!"

For the novice salesman who doesn't know how to blurt out answers to objections right off the bat, remember this: *You don't have to!* Sometimes it is more effective to pause and think for a few moments. It's not only dramatic, but it also shows wisdom and sincere interest in answering the objection. Many salesmen will repeat the question while thinking the answer. This provides an opportunity to think of a good reason to overcome your prospect's objection.

If you are not resourceful in answering objections quickly at first, don't worry. You'll develop the ability in due time.

What Is the Real Objection?

In handling rebuttals, it is vital that the salesman know the *real reason* why his prospect is objecting. Too often, an *excuse* is given by the prospect, rather than the actual reason for his not buying. Without knowing your prospect's real objection, you obviously cannot satisfy his *real* needs.

A fine example of what an "excuse objection" may be is illustrated as follows:

John is trying to convince his good friend, Tom, to take a canoe ride with him. Tom is a non-swimmer and is deeply afraid that the canoe will tip over and he will drown. He has a great fear of drowning but is too embarrassed to admit this to John. Instead, Tom explains that he doesn't like the idea of canoeing in such a dirty, polluted river. No matter how hard John tries to convince Tom that the river is clean and that there is no possibility of water pollution, he cannot persuade his friend that he should not be afraid of drowning and that it is perfectly safe for him to go along in the canoe. Tom's *real* objection—his fear of drowning —will never be answered by John's rebuttals, which are aimed at the question of the river's purity. If John doesn't learn of Tom's real fear—and then deal with it directly—he simply won't have Tom as a canoeing companion.

This example is obvious, but how many times is a salesman in the same boat when he cannot convince a buyer to buy because he is unable to decipher the prospect's *real objection*? If a prospect, for example, states that he "can't afford" to buy—but his real objection is that he doesn't like to deal with "strangers"—think of how slim the possibility is that the salesman can convince him to buy as long as that salesman doesn't realize what the customer is objecting to. All the correct rebuttals in the world on why he "can't afford" to buy will not change the prospect's mind. On the other hand, if the salesman in this example knew his prospect's real objection, he could possibly overcome it through such rebuttals as:

1. Showing proof of the *reputation* of his company. (Testimonial letters are excellent for this purpose.)
2. The salesman's own personal references and background.
3. A list of satisfied customers who could be contacted by the prospect.

The point is that unless the salesman can establish the real reasons for not buying, there is little hope of his getting anywhere by using sales points to satisfy an "excuse objection."

Clues to Look For

There are many signs to look for which will give you clues as to whether your prospect's objection is sincere or false. Sometimes these signs may be hard to discover, but the experienced professional salesman will be able to develop the necessary ability.

The most obvious way of detecting your customer's real objection is by the use of your *natural senses.* As a starter, you should listen very carefully to *what* he says and *how* he says it, and then ask yourself these questions: What does he mean? Why does he say in it this particular way? What is he getting at? Doesn't his hesitation mean that he is looking for an excuse? —and so on. Also, there is much to be gained by carefully analyzing your prospect's reactions—by looking very carefully at his movements and facial expressions. Some people tend to blush or to get nervous—and to fidget, tap their fingers, or fall into other nervous habits. Other people cannot look a salesman squarely in the eye when misstating their real objections. And still others tend to get a nervous sweat. These obvious signs can, in many cases, reveal that your prospect's objections are not valid ones.

Once you are a seasoned salesman, there will be many obvious "excuse objections" that you'll learn to recognize immediately. In all fields of selling, the *stereotyped excuse* may be: I want to think it over! I never buy anything without sleeping on it first! I want to shop around! I never make up my mind on the first call from a salesman! I want to talk it over with my wife (or partner) . . . and so on.

When a buyer says, "I'll take your telephone number and call you when I am ready," this is an obvious sign that you have not yet convinced him of the need so that he may act immediately.

When a customer says, "I want to compare prices with your competitor," he is really saying, "I am not convinced that your product is worth this amount of money."

When a buyer says, "I have to talk it over with my

wife," chances are, he is stalling for time because he is not sold on the need.

Only through experience and alertness will a professional salesman be able to decipher the "excuse objections" from the "real objections."

If too many objections are given, it should be obvious that nobody could have so many different reasons for not wanting your product. Many times, the prospect will give a different objection immediately after you have answered the first one, and then repeat other objections again and again until both the salesman and the customer are confused as to what he is objecting to. Either this prospect doesn't wish to reveal his obvious objections or he just doesn't have the gumption to say "No, I am not interested, I do not want to buy your product!" It is possible that the reason for so many objections is: You have not sold him the need, and thus, have not created the desire to buy. Bring out your big guns. Show him the need. Make him see and feel the need. Convince him! Give him a reason for buying.

Respect Your Prospect's Fair Objections

Naturally, your prospect may have legitimate objections—or just plain good reasons for not buying. Learn and respect these objections and give him a fair answer which he is entitled to hear. If your competition has a selling point that your customer is interested in, don't give excuses why your company does not offer the same feature. Instead, show him what advantages your product has over your competition's. If you are representing a competitive company, then you will have sales points to counteract the strong points of your competition.

Also learn to *respect your prospect's opinions.* A wise salesman realizes that not everybody he calls on thinks exactly like he does. Until you have learned to *respect* your customer's opinions, you will not be able to do an effective job in selling.

S. L. Clemens (Mark Twain) summed it up very well this way: "It is not best that we should all think alike; it is differences of opinion that makes horse-races!"

Once you have learned to respect the other man's opinion, then remember J. R. Lowell's famous quote: "The foolish and the dead alone never change their opinion."

Some Basic Rules in Handling Objections

The following are some basic, common-sense rules in handling your prospect's objections:

1. Do not argue with your prospect. Many times he will be absolutely wrong, but don't tell him so in a blunt manner. Remember, the objective of a sales interview is to make a sale, not to win an argument. The personal satisfaction gained from winning an argument is not nearly as important as the money earned from a sale!

2. Don't ever put your prospect in a position where he has to defend himself or his point of view. Don't embarrass him this way—because, if you

do, he will *fight* you. He will lose sight of the merits of your product and will only be interested in resisting you. In most cases, he will dislike you . . . and people don't like to do business with people they dislike.

3. Never lose your temper. This is a sure way to lose control of the situation and lose a sale. There are many instances where there are reasons for a salesman to lose his temper—but *never good reasons.*

4. Do not interrupt a prospect while he is voicing an objection. It is not only discourteous, but also very annoying. Everybody wants to be listened to. Furthermore, you may find out what he is thinking about. *Listen carefully.*

5. Use the I agree with you, *but* . . . approach. This is an old method but a very successful one where you agree with him—thus winning his confidence—and then you show him why he is wrong. This is an excellent form of diplomacy.

6. Be sure that you understand his objection. If you are not sure, then repeat it like this:

    "Do I understand you to say or mean that . . ." Or, "I don't quite understand what your objection is, Mr. Smith. Would you please repeat it?"

7. Put yourself in your prospect's shoes. In order to understand his objections, you must develop *empathy.*

8. Control the sales interview, but don't become obnoxious and try to browbeat your prospect into being too meek to voice objections. Let him get into the act on occasion. There has to be a two-way system of communication between a salesman and a prospect.

Indecision

There are thousands of reasons why a customer won't buy—and for us to attempt to discuss them individually would be impossible. But the most common reason why the majority of people will not buy is simply *procrastination. They fear making a decision!* Decisions are so painful to some people that they will go to ridiculous lengths just to avoid making them. Probably the biggest reason why a decision of any importance is hard to make is that there is the *risk of being wrong!* It is not a "crime" to be wrong, but many persons act as if it were. How many prospects have you run into who remind you of Buridan's Ass, which starved to death between two stacks of hay because he was unable to decide which was the most desirable?

"As an insurance agent," says Mr. Ed Ellman, "your job is to convince your buyer that taking no action is far more dangerous than taking action! Taking no action when insurance is available can be a form of action that is wrong." Mr. Ellman dramatizes this point to his prospect by saying, "Mr. Friend, one way or another a decision will be made now, even if you think it best to make no decision. You may decide to invest $1,000 into a premium for insurance which proves 'unnecessary' at some later point. In a sense that could be regarded as a $1,000 mistake. While none of us like to make even a $1.00 mistake, your business or your lifestyle will not be altered fundamentally by that sort of a minor mistake. But you may decide to take the action of deferring a decision which really means doing nothing. This might save $1,000 . . . but it could lead to a $100,000 mistake. Tell me, how easy would it be to correct a $100.000 mistake . . . especially if it occurs at the most critical time of your business' existence?"

Many executives will hesitate to make a decision involving something new because their very jobs are at stake. They are afraid to face the consequences if the decision they make is *wrong*. These kinds of executives never stick around long enough to reach top management because little progress can be achieved by people who are afraid to make important decisions. An excellent, thought-provoking rebuttal to this type of buyer is: "Wouldn't it be a sad day for your board of directors to wake up one morning and read in the newspapers that one of your competitors has already decided to go ahead with one of those 'foolish' ideas that you so quickly rejected on first sight?" This type of executive must be made aware of the serious repercussions which will come if he does *not* make a decision to act now. Sell him on the importance of acting now. Point out to him that *procrastination can lead to disaster!*

As Benjamin Franklin put it so wisely: "One today is worth two tomorrows."

Here are a few phrases which indecisive executives will resort to in trying to kill ideas and at the same time make themselves feel justified for their meek actions:

"It's never been done that way before. Why take such a risk now?"

"It won't work in our industry!"

"Too theoretical; not practical!"

"Once, many years ago, we tried it—and it doesn't work!"

"Our stockholders will never accept it."

"If it's such a good idea, our research department would have known about it and recommended it."

"Never swap horses crossing a stream."

The list is endless, but it's the same old story: *indecision!* It is *your job,* as a salesman, to make your prospect aware of his decision-making responsibilities.

Getting a Prospect to Make a Change

Many people will not change from one method of doing things to another, simply because they don't like *change.* It is a sad state of affairs, for people to think in such a biased manner, but it is true!

Mme. Jeanne Roland must have been thinking of the salesman when she said: "The feeble tremble before opinion, the foolish defy it, the wise judge it, and the skillful direct it."

Joe Gandolfo,* who sells over one hundred million dollars of life insurance a year, has the perfect answer to give the prospect who says, "I have enough

*Joe Gandolfo, CLU, *IDEAS ARE A DIME A DOZEN.* page 21; National Underwriters Company

insurance," "I don't believe in life insurance," "I am not interested in discussing insurance with you," etc. Joe simply states, "John, may I ask you a question before I leave? If you'll recall I said that I wanted to share an idea with you. Did you study history in high school or college? You probably recall that during President Adams' administration, Congress came within three votes of abolishing the patent office. It wanted to do away with the patent office because they thought all of the ideas possible had been conceived. It wanted to save the taxpayers' money. But, as you know, since then we've had rockets to the moon, color television, electronic telephones, and who knows what all even here in your business. There is new surgical equipment in the hospital, and new fertilizers and feeds for the farms. The question I would like to ask before I leave is *have you closed your patent office?*" Joe usually gets a reply, "Well, no, not if you look at it that way?"

The skillful salesman knows how to direct his prospect's differences of opinion into thinking positively and acting now. Learn to direct your prospects' opinions toward your own way of thinking. Show them the tremendous advantages of making a change from *Brand X* to your product. Show them that they can only gain by making a change from their old methods to the new methods that your product or service represents.

Convince yourself and convince your prospect of the great service which you are performing for *him* when you help teach him a better way of doing things. This is progress.

Conclusion

There are hundreds of obstacles that you'll encounter in addition to these two most common ones: *Indecision* and the *fear of change.* While these two objections can apply to any and all sales situations in any field, there are many more which will apply to your specific circumstance. It is important, therefore, for you to be aware of all objections which relate to selling your product, and that you have ready-made answers for them. Too many salesmen develop sales presentations and then rush out to make sales calls without learning the art of handling objections. Make sure you have this art down pat along with your sales presentation. It's a one-two punch that gets big production.

Remember, too: Keep calm when your buyer says "NO," and *think* before you answer. Naturally, make sure that you are getting a sincere objection and not a false one. If there are too many objections, then it means you have not created the proper sense of need through your sales presentation. so, begin *again,* and sell him on the need. Show him what it will do for him. Give him a good reason to buy.

Remember that a prospect cannot buy from every salesman he talks to. If he did, he would wind up in the poorhouse. He has built a natural resistance against buying anything except what he *really needs.* So remember: When he says "NO" he is really saying: "Give me some good reasons why I *really need* your product!"

XIV

CONTROL SELLING

Many salesmen believe that once they cease to *control* the sales interview, a sale is lost. Each salesman must realize that he has to be the *commanding force* of a sales interview. Just as the professional actor sets the stage for his audience, so, too, does the professional salesman create a proper climate for his sales interview. "Controlling a prospect" must be done properly at the *beginning* of the sales interview—and it must be conducted in such a subtle way that the prospect is unaware that it is being executed. If it is performed with skill, the salesman will command his prospect's attention. This is one of the skills in selling which must be performed with expert professionalism. It is not for the amateur—but even the amateur must begin developing this technique early in the game, or else he can never hope to become a professional. This chapter will explain the meaning of "control selling" and how you can incorporate it into your own sales interviews.

What Is Control Selling?

Control selling is just what the name implies. It puts the salesman in complete control of the situation. It places him in the "driver's seat" where he can maneuver and chart the buyer's thinking—where he can completely guide the sales interview.

The most effective control selling is accomplished through the *pre-planned sales presentation*. This type of selling (which must be perfectly developed and skillfully mastered) offers an excellent "track" for the salesman to follow. If the salesman's presentation is properly prepared it will follow an order which will give all the facts and at the same time be appealing to the buyer.

One advantage of the planned and control-oriented sales presentation is that interruptions during the sales interview will not confuse the salesman. He will know exactly where he left off before stopping. For instance, if the buyer is interrupted by a telephone call, then when the call is completed, the salesman merely repeats his last point and continues on with his presentation. However, without a pre-planned presentation, it is very likely that a long interruption could make the salesman forget what he had said. In such a case, he may become too repetitious in trying to catch up—and thus, he may bore or annoy his prospect. Or, on the other hand, he may jump ahead too far in his presentation and thus leave out important material.

Another advantage of the pre-planned sales presentation is that it is *complete.* It prevents the omission of important facts by the salesman. By giving complete information, the professional salesman is impressing the buyer with the fact that he is an "expert." The buyer is confident he is dealing with a man who knows exactly what he is talking about—and he feels more assured of the accuracy of the salesman's information. Having confidence in the salesman, the buyer will be less resistant and will find it more pleasant dealing with him.

Perhaps the greatest advantage of control selling is that it develops a *captive audience* for the salesman. The salesman, by knowing his presentation thoroughly, is able to *set the stage*—and by doing so, he knows the exact procedure of the sales interview. He has given the same presentation so many times that he is completely aware of the reactions he might expect of his buyer. By knowing this in advance, he can also pre-plan the method by which he will overcome any obstacles that may come up during the sales interview. What advantage for a salesman to have prepared himself with hard-hitting, proven answers to all of his buyer's objections!

Once he has satisfied his buyer's questions, the professional salesman continues with his sales presentation exactly where he left off. *He never lets the situation get out of his control!*

What Is the Purpose of Control Selling?

The purpose of control selling should be obvious. *Highly effective control selling will guide the thinking patterns of the buyer.* When properly conducted, such a presentation technique will develop patterns òf thought in the prospect's mind and can help the salesman predict how the prospect will think and act. It will also capture the prospect's attention right at the beginning.

Control selling is different from ordinary selling because of the *relationship* that it creates *between the salesman and the buyer.* Instead of a salesman-customer relationship, there will be what one might call a teacher-pupil relationship. In other words, the salesman is placing himself in a more knowledgeable status than his prospect—thus making himself the more important party in the interview. He is no ordinary, run-of-the-mill salesman! This can create the ideal setting for a sales interview. As mentioned before, however, it must be executed properly and *from the very beginning* of the interview if the results are to be properly achieved.

Ordinarily, the average salesman takes the attitude that "the customer is always right." In control selling, however, the professional salesman does *not* start with this premise. He is, of course, *courteous* and *tactful* toward his prospect; but he does *not* assume an ingratiating posture. Instead, he establishes a status of respect for his own expertise. He assumes the role of the expert and of the person who has something of value and something of importance to offer the prospect.

The big advantage of control selling becomes most obvious when it is time to *close* the sale. Having conditioned the buyer to think in a given pattern, the professional salesman finds it relatively easy at this point to "guide" him into buying. If the salesman had proper control during the first stages of the sales interview, it will be a fairly routine matter for him to show the prospect *how to buy*. (The closing of a sale is discussed in detail in the following chapter.)

Little-Known Methods of Controlling the Buyer

It was previously mentioned that a relationship similar to that of the teacher and pupil is established during the interview when the salesman is getting *control* of his buyer's attention. There are many subtle and little-known methods by which this kind of relationship can be developed. Some of these are:

1. "Mr. Prospect, I want you to sit over here, and Mrs. Prospect, you take this seat right beside your husband. It is very important that you *see*, as well as *listen*, to what I have to show you." (This is a fine example of a salesman controlling his prospects immediately with a simple courteous "order" as to what he wants them to do.)

2. "Mrs. Prospect, I would appreciate it if you were to get me a cold glass of water." (Here, the salesman is giving the prospect's wife an unassuming order which, naturally, she will politely obey.)

3. "Mrs. Prospect, feel the fine fabric that this material is made of." (Another unpretentious *direct* order during a sales interview.)

4. "Mr. Prospect, I want you to pay close attention to this feature. Move a little closer so you can see exactly what I am going to demonstrate to you." (The buyer automatically moves closer, unconsciously obeying a simple order which the salesman has given him.)

5. "Mr. Prospect, I am now going to permit you to operate this machine by yourself. I want you to do exactly what I tell you." (Once again, the prospect is having his thoughts and actions *guided by the salesman!*)

These "little orders" don't seem like they have much meaning at the time when they are given, but they *condition the buyer to do as the salesman says.* Then, at the point when the salesman is ready to close the sale the buyer is so accustomed to obeying the salesman's "little orders" that he automatically obeys when he is handed a pen and told, "Just put your ok right here on the dotted line." At this point, it is also a conditioned reaction for him to obey what the salesman next requests: "Please make your check payable for the full amount to the company."

Conclusion

It is vitally important that you develop this technique of *control selling* if you wish to become a *professional* salesman. It requires *four basic elements* which every professional salesman should automatically possess:

1. Self-confidence
2. Complete product knowledge
3. A definite, pre-planned sales presentation
4. Practice . . . and perfect timing!

Control selling will be easy once a salesman possesses these qualities . . . and his selling will be much more rewarding too!

XV

THE CLOSE
(THE MONEY-MAKER)

"Salesmen don't get paid for talking to prospects
. . . they get paid for selling (closing) them!"

Let's face it: Unless you close a sale, you really
aren't selling. After all, a sales interview is only an
exchange of ideas—until you close the sale with an
exchange of *money!* You will never be a big money-
maker in the sales field until you have mastered the art
of successful closing. Pay special attention to this
chapter—learning how to close a sale will ultimately
put money in your pocket.

Every salesman surely realizes that although a
prospect may have a definite need (and desire) for his
product, more often than not, there exists a noticeable
reluctance to part with his money when it is time to
buy. In most cases, this is true because the average
buyer has *many* needs but only *limited* financial re-

sources to fulfill them. He may think: "I certainly can't buy everything. Is this really the most value which I can get for my money?" Sure, he may like your product—but what will make him buy it? Certainly, a good presentation or demonstration can illustrate the advantages, but it is the *effective close* which creates desire *to take action to buy now!*

Nothing is more imperative for a salesman to realize than the immediate necessity of a strong, persuasive close. If selling is going to be your livelihood, the effective close, by and large, is going to be the determining factor dictating how much money you will earn. Remember: Commissions are only paid when a sale is closed; you don't earn a penny until then! Make selling a profitable venture, as it is so rightly intended to be. Make it your business to be a great closer! It's a pity when a prospect is given sound selling reasons to buy, and the salesman lacks the ability to close the sale! Too often, this is the case.

The Key Word Is "Confidence"

Above all, you must close a sale with complete confidence! Perhaps no other single factor in your behavior will more greatly influence your buyer's opinion of you. This chapter will highlight some of the many closing techniques, but always remember: Every close must be executed with supreme confidence. This is the common denominator which every successful salesman possesses, regardless of the closing technique he employs. To close a sale without it will be fruitless—it is a must! Confidence means quality.

Confidence flashes a subliminal message into your buyer's mind. It tells him: "This salesman is confident because he enjoys great success in selling his product! If everybody buys then it must be good!" A lack of confidence, on the other hand, produces doubt in your prospect's mind. He may think: "There must be something wrong with the product because the salesman's lack of confidence means he doesn't expect me to buy! I better be careful. Something's wrong . . . I don't think the product is all it's cracked up to be. I better not buy now until I find out what's what . . ."

Confidence Shows Sincerity

What is the first impression that you get of a person who can't look you straight in the eye? *Insincerity.* Right? The salesman who lacks confidence will generally leave his prospect with the impression: "What's this guy trying to get away with? He must be hiding something!" The salesman who lacks confidence will produce doubt, nervousness and suspicion in his prospect's mind. He will appear as though he doesn't believe in his product himself. On the other hand, the confident salesman will flash an opposite subliminal message: "Now, this salesman really believes what he is saying!" Confidence and conviction are one of a kind.

Confidence Means Success

The mere fact that a salesman is full of confidence is positive proof of his success. On the other hand, the down-and-outer who knows nothing but failure shows the tell-tale signs which accompany being a loser. People like to deal with successful people. Failure breeds failure. Success breeds success.

Confidence Is Contagious

The weak salesman who hems and haws during his close will find his prospect reacting in the same manner when it's time for a final "yes or no." Those hems and haws will be as contagious as a yawn! And the prospect will catch the "Disease." He'll say that he has to "think it over for a few days." In other words, the salesman who lacks confidence during his close will infect his prospects with hesitation, boredom and negativism.

The salesman who lacks confidence will constantly get negative results at the close of his sale. The usual excuses will be: "I never make a decision on the spur of the moment." "I have to talk it over with my wife (or partner) before I can make up my mind." "I have to shop your competitors before I make a decision." "I just don't know . . ." etc. Timid excuses will be given to timid salesmen. The meek salesman brings out meekness in his prospects.

On the other hand, when you are acting as the

buyer, don't you find it embarrassing to give a weak excuse to a strong, persuasive man? While it may be easy to act that way with "Mr. Milquetoast," you simply don't behave that way with the dynamic, forceful salesman.

Your prospect will definitely be influenced by your personality. *Confidence and hesitation are contagious! Which one are you spreading amongst your prospects?*

Remember: Positive thoughts produce positive action. Confidence is the most vital element required to achieve success.

The "Major-Minor" Closing Technique

This is basically one of the most easily managed closing techniques, and it will get excellent results immediately. It works on every type of prospect, regardless of age, income, occupation or sex. This method, when perfectly executed, will depend on perfect timing; yet it is quite simple to develop and easy for the beginner to learn.

The major-minor close gives you a track to run on, and it can be learned quickly by an outline form. It is a sure-fire, step-by-step procedure which shows the prospect how to buy.

Just how does the major-minor closing technique work? We all know that the average buyer has a difficult time making a *major* decision. Yet we also know that it's not hard for him to make a *minor* one. Well, the major-minor close does exactly that. It allows the buyer to make several minor decisions which, in effect, add up to a *major* one.

A good example is the life insurance agent who knows that his prospect isn't capable of making a big decision such as, "Yes, I'll buy this policy and pay your company $2,000 each year until I reach age 65." Such a commitment on the part of the buyer is too big an obligation for him to decide on the spur of the moment. With this in mind, the experienced life insurance agent allows his buyer to make little decisions (minor ones) which take little thinking to agree. "Shall I put down your wife as your beneficiary?" The buyer can quickly answer "yes" to that question. Then another question is asked which demands a minor answer: "Would you like to handle this on a monthly basis?" The prospect answers, "Why yes, that's how I pay for all of my insurance and mutual funds." Next, the salesman asks, "Shall we have the home office send the premiums to your residence?" Obviously, it takes very little effort for the buyer to decide on such a minor point. Before the buyer knows it, he has made a decision to buy on the basis of a series of smaller decisions. He has not had the burden of having to make a major one.

A great many people are unable to make what they consider a major decision. For this reason, such persons will resort to any means available to keep from being put on the spot and to keep from being forced to act now on a major issue. A professional salesman who incorporates the major-minor close into his sales presentation with this type of buyer is doing him a great service. The prospect wants to make a major decision, and the salesman is helping him to do so by directing his decision-making to only minor issues. Quite often, he may actually feel relieved because the salesman has made his task easy.

Remember: Ten *minor* decisions are ten times easier to make than one *major* one.

A Simple Close When Answering Objections

Suppose you're working on a difficult close, and you take the following approach with your prospect:

"Do I understand you correctly, Mr. Prospect, that this is your *only* objection for not buying? You agree that everything else is perfect? And, furthermore, you would buy immediately if it were not for *(Prospect's Objection)?*"

Once your prospect has said "yes" to this, then he is backed into a corner. And if you can then give him a thorough, exact answer to his one remaining objection, he has no other excuses. He should then be closed quite simply.

The secret of this close is to first obtain a definite commitment from your prospect that he will buy if you can satisfactorily answer his "only" objection for not buying now.

The "Limited Offer" Technique

We are all familiar with the limited offer technique which we see in everyday living. Examples are the newspaper ads stating, "Only one to a customer—Thursday only" . . . or, "Weekend Special—car wash only 99¢."

Obviously, the purpose of such promotions is to stimulate sales by offering a bargain for only a *limited period*. Such selling creates an "emergency" to buy now at special values.

When it is available, the limited offer technique is a very effective method of closing a sale. The automobile salesman may say, "Mr. Smith, I will give you a special price on this last year's Buick only because I want to make room for the new ones! This is the last one we have in this model, and once this baby is sold, we'll be completely out of them forever!" Knowing his customer is only interested in purchasing the last year's model at a lower price, the salesman has created "fear" in his buyer's mind that if he doesn't buy now (during the limited time available) he'll lose the chance to buy this particular bargain altogether.

The limited offer technique is also quite effective in selling real estate. The alert real estate broker often puts the pressure on his client by saying, "I know how much you appreciate this house, but I also have two other families who are almost certain to be bidding on it in the next day or two. I'm sure that one of them will buy this house if they have the chance, so I'm afraid you might lose out if we don't submit a bid right now."

A word of caution: If you are going to use the limited offer technique, be absolutely certain that you can logically back it up. If you are bluffing, and your buyer calls you on it, you'll lose the sale— and, in some cases, you may even find yourself facing legal problems.

The "special offer" technique (which the limited offer technique is sometimes called) is particularly effective with the prospect who can't make up his mind —the type of prospect who always wishes to delay or postpone a decision. He may want your product, but it takes a little extra pushing for him to reach a decision. However, you should also be aware of the danger of *too much pressure*. Often, the prospect can be pushed to the point where he resents it—where he may begin to think of you as a "high-pressure" salesman.

Let's assume, though, that you are alert and skillful in applying just the right amount of pressure—but you still haven't made the close. This is the perfect spot for the "special offer." Your first close has failed, and it is time to offer a further inducement to *buy now*. This is where the special offer comes to your rescue. It brings a new flavor to the situation. It tells your prospect that only by acting now can he gain an immediate advantage, and the lack of immediate action will mean a *loss* to him.

The special offer is always a small consideration, but it represents something *free!* Items worth only a few cents have tipped the scales of sales involving thousands of dollars. For example, the kitchen salesman will produce many extra sales by offering a free kitchen clock "if you sign the contract today, since we have only a few clocks left!"

The successful book salesman will offer a reference book to his customer if he signs today. The reference book may only cost a dollar, but it gets him sale after sale of encyclopedias worth $300.00 each.

A very successful sweeper salesman told this book's authors that every time a prospect tried to put off buying, and he knew that the prospect *really wanted* a sweeper, he would offer a free plastic cover for the machine if the customer bought today. The plastic covers only cost him 50 cents each, but he said that you would have thought they were worth $20.00 the way this special offer worked!

Assuming the Sale

This is one of the smoothest and easiest methods used in closing a sale. Perhaps more sales are made through this simple method than through all of the other closes combined.

If you are satisfied that your presentation has run smoothly, then you simply take it for granted that your prospect has decided to buy, and you start writing up the order. In many cases, no other selling is needed.

The television salesman, for example, may "assume" the sale by asking, "Will somebody be at your home on Monday morning to receive this set?" Although the prospect hasn't actually said that he definitely will buy the TV, he may find himself responding almost automatically. "Why yes," he says. "Monday morning would be fine." And by saying so, he has made a commitment to buy.

The jeweler who notices the fiancée slipping one diamond ring on and off her finger repeatedly, says, "I think you made an excellent choice, Miss. What are your initials? I'll have them engraved on the inside of the band." By giving her initials, she is saying, "We decided to buy this one!"

John Berglas,* a nationally-known life insurance producer, would simply assume the sale by saying, "Would you prefer to have the premium sent to your home or to your office?" John claims that when his client would indicate which address he preferred to use as a mailing address it was the same as saying, "Yes, I'll buy a policy from you."

Another example might be the men's clothing salesman. After having his customer try on a suit which is picked from the rack, he might say, "How do you like it?" And as quickly as he gets an affirmative answer, he *assumes* the sale by starting to measure the length of the jacket and making chalk marks on the sleeves and trousers. By allowing him to continue, the customer is saying, in effect, "OK, I decided to buy this suit!"

"Assuming the sale" is a selling method which can be used effectively by every salesman. But, *if it doesn't work the first time, then keep selling and close again.*

"Green-Light" Buying Signals

It is essential that you be able to recognize *when* it is time to close the sale. There are certain "green-light" buying signals that can help you in doing this.

---

*John Berglas, President, Planned Equity Corporation. In 1972 Mr. Berglas' company sold over $200 million of life insurance.

You should learn to recognize them, because there is a danger in *over-selling*—in going past the moment when the customer is actually ready to buy.

Green-light buying signals are flashed in two ways: by *words* or by *actions*. Certain questions or comments can be obvious word signals. But, many times, action signals are difficult to recognize. For example, a customer may be watching a salesman demonstrate a water-proof and shock-proof wristwatch. The salesman puts the watch into a jar of water for a few minutes and then drops it on the counter. (This, of course, is showmanship with a *plus!*) While he is doing this, he is explaining the many features of his product. "This watch will wind automatically without the slightest movement of your wrist," says the salesman, swinging the watch back and forth. "It really winds easily, doesn't it?" All this time, the customer remains silent. "This watch," the salesman continues, "is 100 percent water-proof and shock-proof, and it is also anti-magnetic. It has been adjusted and tested to keep split-second time." The customer still hasn't uttered a word, but the salesman continues to explain: "This watch has a ratchet arrangement attached to the pendulum which swings back and forth with the slightest movement of your arm. When the mainspring is fully wound, the ratchet gear locks the winding mechanism, and the pendulum winds the ratchet, which is temporarily disengaged from the mainspring until the mainspring unwinds to a point where the ratchet gear releases and permits the ratchet to go to work again and wind the spring. The spring can never overwind." The salesman puts the watch on the counter, and his customer—still silent—picks up the watch, fastens it on his arm, and swings it back and forth. A smile of satisfaction comes on his face. *The green-light buying signal has flashed on!* This is the *sign* the salesman was waiting for, and he closes the sale!

Like the watch salesman, you must be alert to every buying signal a customer gives you. When a customer handles an article, examines it or demonstrates it, you should realize that he is interested. These are the *silent* green-light buying signals.

The *word* signals are usually questions expressing an interest such as, "Is it guaranteed?" "Can I get good financing terms?" "What colors does it come in?" . . . and so on.

Whenever you think that the green-light buying signal has flashed, it's time for you to close the sale. If it really *hasn't* flashed, then continue with the sales presentation and wait for a more opportune time to try again for your close.

Conclusion

You must be skilled in all of the closing techniques discussed in this chapter if you want to achieve success in selling. Learn *all* of the closes; *practice* them diligently; and incorporate the proper close into your sales presentation so that you can meet any situation that arises during a sale.

The close should be practiced repeatedly until perfect timing is achieved. In fact, it should be practiced more than any other phase of the selling process —and for two reasons: First, because it is used the *least;* you don't get an opportunity to give the close to every prospect because you are often stopped midway in your presentation or at the three-quarter mark. Therefore, your close is very apt to be your weakest selling point! Second, if your presentation was not up to par at the ending, a strong close can still overcome most objections. On the other hand, an otherwise fine sales presentation with an ineffective close accomplishes nothing. You must *close* the sale to earn your salary or commission. The proof of ability is results. In the sales field, the result is the *sale*.

XVI

EXTRA AMMUNITION

Every professional salesman must have *reserves* available to use when the going gets tough! This is often what separates the men from the boys. In many cases, after a sales presentation has been given, the buyer is not quite convinced he should buy. These borderline cases, where the buyer is "on the fence," are the ones which the true *pros* always close. They make the difference between a top producer and a run-of-the-mill salesman. The professional salesman gets them every time. Why? . . .Because the professional salesman has *extra ammunition,* and the mediocre salesman doesn't.

A top-flight salesman will have *reserve strength*—just like a big time football team must have. Study the championship teams throughout the years, and you will note that every one of them has been known for having a strong "bench." In fact, the subs are usually on a par with the first team and with would-be starters on the other teams in the league.

The professional salesman, too, must have "bench strength." He must have that *extra* set of resources—the extra "ammunition"—which can make the real difference at the close.

After all, the *close* is the time when a salesman has to be at his *strongest.* The *ordinary* salesman is usually weakest at this point, but the *professional* salesman is just beginning to gather momentum. He's determined to get the sale. Nothing is going to stop him now! And usually nothing will!

Having complete *product knowledge* is certainly one way to always be well equipped. Perhaps it may be necessary to explain *other* facets of your product which you haven't mentioned up until the close. It may be that these added features are the *extra ammunition* which will give your prospect a needed push and close your sale. Perhaps you have held back on a product demonstration—but at the close is when you give it. Or, it may be that you haven't let your prospect "get into the act"—until closing time, when you finally let him actually handle or use the product for the first time.

Be resourceful and give your customer *another purpose* for buying—a purpose which will seem to him to be different from all the other reasons you have offered before.

The Third-Person Story

There's a Latin saying which goes: "Exemplum Decets." Translated, it means, "The example teaches." Use this ancient wisdom; it still applies significantly today.

Perhaps nothing is more powerful than a third-person story at the right time. It may be that your buyer doesn't need any more "product knowledge" at the closing point in your presentation—but what he needs is to see an actual case history of how your product has benefited another buyer. THIS CASE HISTORY MIGHT VERY WELL HAVE BEEN HIM! Tell it to him convincingly, and give him exact details. Third-person stories paint a much more vivid picture of what your product actually does than any other single technique you may use in a sales presentation.

A third-person story is used very successfully in "intangible" selling. A good life insurance agent will always have several third-person stories in reserve. Perhaps after all of the figures are spread all over the dining room table, and all of the insurance policy's benefits have been fully explained, the prospect is still not in a buying mood. At this point, the top-flight life insurance salesman will add, "Tom, I'm sure that you know Jim Gibson's family down the street, don't you?" Tom shakes his head and stutters, "Do you mean the young widow and four kids who live at 1515 Elm Street? Why those poor kids!" The salesman nods his head and continues, "Jim was only 34 years old when he had his heart attack and had never been sick or hurt a day in his life! I remember when he told me that he didn't need life insurance because all his family lived to old ages. He was just one of those fellows who didn't believe in insurance. In fact, he didn't have *one red cent* of life insurance! It's hard to believe in this day and age that there are people who think like that, isn't it?" Tom, naturally, agrees. Then the salesman continues: "Tom, do you know that it was only three months after I talked to Jim that he died?" He pauses for a few seconds and whispers, "It doesn't seem possible that such a strong, well-developed young man could collapse on the golf course like that. He only lived for about two hours before he died. They rushed him to City Hospital, but his wife arrived about twenty minutes too late. She was out shopping and nobody could locate her in time. And, as you know, when I went to his funeral, I could hardly look her straight in the eye, because I felt partly responsible for Jim's not taking out that policy. She was all for it, but he wouldn't budge; and she told me later at the house that she had no idea what they were going to do for money. She used up all of their savings for the funeral, and she isn't prepared to get a job with her lack of experience. That poor girl doesn't know what to do. And really, there's not much hope at this point. The time to have made preparations was when I visited with Jim *before* he suffered his heart attack. It's always too late to take out life insurance when you finally need it."

Tom then asks, "How much insurance do you think my family should have in addition to what I now carry?"

The third-person story has worked perfectly!

This particular example is one of many similar techniques that the top life insurance salesman will use. It is an example of a prospect's tragic mistake and the suffering he caused because he did not buy the product. It vividly illustrates the consequences if the prospect does not buy.

Another good third-person story is one in which you can demonstrate how a smart buyer profited from a purchase. For example, a mutual fund salesman might say, "Mr. Jones, have you ever wondered how Mr. Young, who works in the same department as you, enjoys such a higher standard of living? After all, he belongs to the country club, has two cars and a swimming pool, and goes on expensive vacations every year." Mr. Jones sighs, "I always figured he must have inherited a lot of money." Then he laughs, "Or he hit the numbers!" The salesman explains, "The truth is that he has made a fortune with his mutual fund investment over the past twelve years. I brought Mr. Young into this fund with the idea that he might save up enough money to send his two daughters to college. But what happened is another story! Not only did he accumulate enough for their college educations, but he also became a wealthy man in the process." The salesman then pulls out the charts which show the growth of *XYZ Fund* over the past twelve years and adds, "Here it is in black and white. This chart tells the whole story of the fantastic growth of this company. It's my firm opinion that the next twelve years are going to be even more fantastic." Mr. Jones, at this point, should be responding. Hopefully, he'll say something like, "I've got to do something about this right away. Why, it's a disgrace how I've neglected saving on my high income over the years. Put me down for the same plan Mr. Young has!"

The third-person story does something that nothing else will do. It shows *actual proof* of how somebody benefited from a purchase. It also shows proof of the disasters which can happen to a prospect if he does *not*.

When you tell a *good* third-person story be sure to paint a vivid picture and use details. This helps your prospect identify with the other person, and he becomes *the person* in the story. He sees this happening to *him*. If you give a detailed picture, he will put himself in the shoes of the third person.

Here are a few tips on how to tell good third-person stories:

1. Always use *real* names, places, ages, etc. Never tell a story like this: "Well, this guy from another town. . ." If you do not use a detailed illustration, then the buyer cannot properly associate himself with the other person.

2. Use a case history with similarities to your prospect's own situation. If you associate your third person in the story with your prospect, he will better identify himself as "that person."

3. Don't be afraid to tell a *long story*. If time is not an important factor, then give your buyer a long story. Everybody is interested in listening to a good, long story. . .if it's told well.

4. Tell a good story. Practice your third-person stories like you practice your sales presentation. If you tell a good, interesting story, your buyer will respond to it accordingly. Nothing is worse than a poorly told story. If you're going to tell one

... tell a good one. Practice using dramatics when you tell it. Give good facts and figures. Be convincing.

5. Be dramatic. Appeal to the emotions of your buyer. Nothing in selling can appeal to the buyer's emotions more powerfully than the third-person story.

The Testimonial Letter

In many cases, the endorsement of a testimonial letter will have more influence on a sale than any other single force or method you can use. As the name suggests, a testimonial letter is a recommendation by a satisfied customer who highly approves of the quality of either: (1) the product; (2) the company; (3) the salesman; or (4) any combination of all. It is the stamp of approval, a form of guarantee by an impartial party *who has actually used the product.* The testimonial letter also has a special advantage because *it is in writing!* The written word—with a man's signature—is undeniable, conclusive proof! It is a bona fide confirmation of customer satisfaction . . . it cannot be argued because it is in writing. Many professional salesmen collect dozens of these letters over the years and they are not bashful when it comes to showing them off.

The testimonial letter is very effective on the "doubting Thomas" prospect. This type of person wants to buy, but he must be thoroughly convinced of the truth of your claims. He is very cautious, perhaps because he has been "burned" before. . .and he won't let it happen to him again. A letter or two written by prominent citizens in the community will have a great deal of influence on this type of prospect.

For example, Jack Harris, a sales manager for a large real estate firm, is undecided about enrolling his twenty salesmen in the *Business and Professional College of Public Speaking's* Thursday evening classes. Jack says, "Three hundred dollars per man is a lot of money for such a large sales force like mine. I've seen this kind of course before, and they don't seem to cut the mustard! I've taken three courses myself with other companies—and it was money down the drain! I'd be willing to give a thousand dollars per man if the course would get results. It's worth it to me if our production goes up as a result of the course."

Don Smith, the salesman, breaks out in a big grin, "Look Jack," he says. "I couldn't agree with you more! Being in this field, I've seen a hundred of those 'phony' courses that turn out to be a waste of time and money. But don't take my word for it." As he hands him a letter he says, "Here, read this."

January 30, 1968

Mr. Donald Smith
Business & Professional
College of Public Speaking
100 Main Street
Pittsburgh, Pennsylvania

Dear Don:

Again, let me thank you for your fine services. I still can't get over the tremendous increase in our sales during the second half of 1967 after our sales force completed your excellent course on public speaking. And, do you realize that the second half of the year is normally our *slow* season? But, this time around, it was different. We never had such a good six months at any time of the year.

I owe you a special "thanks" for convincing me that we should *even take the course*. I was completely against it, thinking that it was like all of the others. It only took me a few phone calls to your satisfied clients to prove to me that it would work!

Your outstanding program made a firm believer out of me. I highly recommend your company, The Business and Professional College of Public Speaking, to all sales organizations who have problems in motivating their salesmen. You may use this letter as testimony if you wish. Or, better yet, Don, have 'em give me a call. I'll show you what a salesman I turned out to be.

Best regards. Don't forget to call on us again this year.

Sincerely,

Edward Scott
President

ES/rw

"I also have another letter for you to read, Jack," Don gleams. But Jack doesn't even bother. "Never mind. If Ed Scott feels that way about it, then sign me up!"

Only the name has been changed on the following letter which was actually received:

November 14,1972

Mr. Martin Rosenberg
3004-B Overton Drive
Greensboro, North Carolina 27408

Dear Marty:

Ironically, I found your brochure of the fine long-term disability policy in my desk drawer this morning. Had I not been "too busy" and evasive, and had you been more persistent, I would be insured today. As you know, I have been disabled with a heart attack for eight months already. According to my doctor, I might not ever go back to work.

I realize that I can't qualify for the policy now, but perhaps this note will urge someone else to act while he has his good health. My procrastination cost me thousands of dollars. . .

Thanks anyway.

Sincerely,

Austin Lackey

Notice that this letter tells the message of how the prospect can suffer if he does not buy! A successful life underwriter is well aware of the tremendous impact of such testimonial letters.

Top producers are generally resourceful salesmen who keep many testimonial letters on hand for the right occasions. After proper sizing-up of a prospect, they show the "ideal" testimony which is most appropriate for each situation. These testimonial letters are excellent sales aids and should be in the portfolio of every salesman. If you haven't received any letters by mail, then visit some of the customers with whom you enjoy a very close relationship, and ask them how how they feel about: (1) your company; (2) your product; (3) your service; and (4) *you*. Assuming that you chose the right ones, you should receive praise and sincere compliments. Ask them if they would like to do you a special favor and put down their sentiments in writing. If their comments are genuine, then they will be delighted to do you a favor. (If you cannot find any customers who will cooperate, then somewhere you have failed—or you are with the wrong company.) If necessary, help the customer write the letter on his letter-head. And be sure to have approval in writing from each customer allowing you to show the letter.

For the beginners: Don't worry! If you do a conscientious job, you soon will receive plenty of testimonial letters.

Conclusion

As the Boy Scouts always say, "Be prepared." In selling, *be prepared with extra ammunition.* Remember that selling is a law-of-averages business, and in many cases, you can "get by" without the *extra ammunition.* But if you want to increase your production by raising your law of averages, then "be prepared." *Have re-serves.* Sure, you'll probably manage to get by some-how without the reserves. So do top football teams— *until one of their starters gets injured!* As demonstrated, with the proper ammunition like third-person stories and testimonial letters, it's quite simple to give your sales presentation a powerful one-two punch when you need it! That extra wallop has influenced many prospects to buy *now* instead of waiting. It's the differ-ence between a *few* sales and *top* production.

XVII

LISTENING IS PART OF EFFECTIVE SELLING

"Silence is one great art of conversation."
. . . *Hazlitt*

One of America's favorite myths is the stereotype of the "supersalesman." This myth has been perpetuated in fiction, in song, on the stage, on film, and at countless cocktail parties. It pictures the salesman as a glib, fast-talking, sometimes hypnotic personality. And it often credits him with abnormal charm, finesse, and eloquence.

Above all, it shows him *talking* . . . constantly talking. It attributes to him even greater lung-power than the country preacher or the carnival barker.

But, like many myths, this picture is an exaggeration based on a *norm*. It shows that a lot of salesmen probably *do* talk a lot—and probably too much.

Of course, effective salesmanship *does* require skill in communicating . . . skill in persuasiveness. But, communicating is a two-way process; and persuasion requires a knowledge of what the other person thinks and feels and wants.

Therefore, a professional salesman has to be just as skillful at *listening* as he is at *talking*.

"LISTEN: BUT HOW?"

How do you begin to listen? Simply by being alert and trying to *observe.* Listen to the comments your prospect is making. *Analyze* them. What is he saying? Don't allow his words to go in one ear and out the other. Hear them out, and be conscious of what he is *really* saying. Digest the thoughts, and then THINK! And—always watch for the "need signals" . . . the "buying signals" in what he is saying. Don't try to overwhelm him with a rote presentation.

Once you have done your listening there is always the opportunity for you to respond. Naturally, you have to use good judgment to respond properly—but, if you haven't really heard what he's been saying, then good judgment is not even possible.

A good example of listening might be illustrated by the automobile salesman who hears his prospect's wife say: "Honey, did you see the Miller's new Mercedes? Gee, that Bob Miller must be making a fortune!"

The *experienced* auto salesman will take this comment to mean that the prospect and his wife are very status-conscious—and he will build his sales presentation around this point. In other words, he will have picked up a buying signal. Another example might involve the electronic calculating machine salesman who picks up a big clue when his prospect asks, "How much more time will your presentation take? I never like to spend too much time with a salesman." The salesman realizes that his prospect places a high value on time, and so he might respond by saying, "Mr. Quick, this new model will save your company a lot of time. In fact, it will save several times what it costs over the period of a year. Our printout saves 5 or 6 seconds every time you total it, as compared to the adding machine you're using now. Those seconds will become hours—hours which your people save!"

As you can see, a salesman might be too busy talking to do some effective listening. But, many times, it's the *listening* that will give him the *signal* which will ultimately lead to a sale.

It's really so simple! All you have to do is pay attention to what your prospect is saying!

Does the Prospect Always Mean What He Says?

Effective listening will tell you many things that aren't quite what they sound like on the surface. (Does this seem like "double talk?" If it does, then remember how many times you *thought* that you heard something—but it turned out you heard wrong.)

What a person *says* and what a person *means* are often worlds apart. And what is left *unsaid* can many times be the most important part of a message.

For example, if a prospect tells a life insurance

agent, "I never heard of your company . . . I want to think it over before I make a decision to buy," the agent may have some doubts about what his prospect has just said. He may be associated with one of the major insurance companies in the nation, and it doesn't make any sense to him that his prospect "never heard of it." Thus, knowing that his prospect can't seriously have any doubts about his company, he has to look for the meaning behind the comment. And, in the meantime, it would be wasteful, if not foolish, to launch into a long presentation on his company's status and credentials. What this salesman needs to do is consider what other factors might be negatively influencing his prospect. All the conversation in the world about the company's financial strength won't offer an effective response to the prospect's *apparent* objection.

A novice salesman might become discouraged when his prospect comes at him like a bear and shouts: "I swore that I'd throw out the next salesman who came in that door . . . I can't stand salesmen!" While this novice would quickly make a beeline for the door, the *experienced* salesman would realize that this type of prospect has very little sales-resistance and can't say "no" to salesmen. Very often this type of prospect can be quite unnerving to speak with because of his outward resistance. But, if you *listen*— and look behind what he's saying, you might find that he is merely putting up a defense barrier because he's unsure of himself. The *professional* salesman—instead of backing away at first sight of this barrier—would try to get

his example illustrates: If you don't listen
you can completely overlook the ammuni-
need to make the sale.

lusion

g is totally dependent upon the art of com-
n. And, since communication is a two-way
ing also is a two-way street. It rests not only
g, but also upon listening.

ing is just as essential to effective selling as
other selling tools discussed in this book.
ing if you're not already doing so—and
ver a new dimension in selling. You'll be-
rstand your prospect better. You'll become
e of his needs and his motivations. Once
ens, your results will surely improve.
e, you'll also *enjoy* selling more than ever.
sten.

behind it and find out what the prospect's *real* motivation or *real* objection is.

Listening to Objections

The first rule in listening to objections is to give
your prospect the *courtesy of listening!* Nothing is more
impolite than the salesman who won't listen. If nothing else, it's a matter of just plain good manners.

Secondly, if your prospect recognizes that you are
really listening to him, he will sense that you have a
sincere interest in him. Certainly, he should respect you
for this, and he will realize that you are not just trying
to sell to him for a short-term or one-shot personal
gain. If he believes that you have his best interest in
mind—and that you are attempting to build a satisfied
and perhaps long-term customer relationship—he will
be more likely to cooperate with you. On the other
hand, if he feels that your main interest is a "quick"
commission, then he may be likely to resist you, and
the sale will be lost! So, perhaps just as important as
the *actual* listening is the *appearance* of listening. Just
as *you* like to be "listened to," so also does your prospect!

When listening to objections, also make sure that
you understand *what* your prospect is objecting to. If
you are not sure, merely ask him politely to repeat his
objection. This gives him further evidence of your
seriousness, and it gives you time to digest and understand his meaning.

Always remember that you must know what the *real* objection is. And the best way to discover it is by listening.

It is extremely important to develop the art of listening with your long-term or "repeat" customers. These are the people who can build a strong sales base for you and provide you with a "satisfied customer" list that can mean so much in developing new sales. In other words, make them *know* that you're truly interested in them by *listening to what they have to say.*

Ask "Why?"

One of the most effective ways to handle objections is to ask "Why?" And then listen *for the answer.* Let your prospect *answer his own objection!*

For example, when selling automobile tires, the alert salesman will ask the indecisive customer, "Why don't you want to buy a set of tires today?"

Then, he remains absolutely silent until the customer replies, "Well, I don't like to make quick decisions."

Next, the salesman might ask, "But don't you need to replace your bald tires today?"

"Well," says the customer, "I guess I *should.* My tires scare the heck out of me when I'm on the freeway . . . especially on a rainy day."

At this, the salesman asks, "Why don't you get rid of the worry, then? Why should you keep yourself up-tight when it's so easy to do something about it?"

Listen for Clues

Good listening will ena[...] prospect and close the sal[...] you'll detect what closing te[...] bring the sale in. As discus[...] are various techniques for [...] of which one you should [...] pend on how well you hav[...]

Furthermore, decidin[...] MUNITION, as discussed [...] be done through good lis[...]

The same thing wou[...] letters. When Mr. Smith a[...] the results you guarante[...] show him testimonial lett[...] But, if he hadn't *listene[...]* missed a golden opportu[...] objection.

The life insurance a[...] listener. For one thing, [...] should use an emotion[...] one. If his prospect m[...] unusual level of concer[...] will aim his appeal at th[...] impulses. For example[...] mostly concerned abo[...] plete college educatio[...] tional appeal than is t[...] about estate taxes!

As [...] properly [...] tion you[...]

Con[...]

Selli[...] municati[...] street, se[...] upon *tell[...]*

Liste[...] any of th[...] Try liste[...] you'll dis[...] gin to unc[...] more awa[...] this happ[...] Chances a[...] *It pays to [...]*

XVIII

SELLING "INTANGIBLES"

Many salesmen misunderstand the challenge of selling *intangibles*. Too many feel that selling the intangible product is far more difficult than selling tangible or concrete ones. This, of course, is absurd—and it can only be a misconception shared by amateurs.

It is the purpose of this chapter to inform the rank-and-file salesman about the fast-growing field of intangible selling, and perhaps open a new dimension to his sales career.

First, let's discuss the obvious reasons why so many salesmen believe that tangible products are easier to sell than intangibles:

1. The *tangible* product can be presented by appealing to the *five senses*. The prospect can *see, feel, hear, smell* or *taste* the product. It is of a material, concrete nature. And generally, a *combination* of the physical senses can be affected or appealed to during the sales presentation. With the *intangible*

product, however, the salesman has nothing concrete or physical that the prospect can look at, handle, listen to, smell or taste.

2. The purchase of a tangible product represents getting an "exchange for your money." It is something "physical" and can be enjoyed or utilized immediately. An *intangible* product, however, can only offer a *promise* that the purchaser will be given an exchange for his money in the future.

3. Because of points one and two (above), it is deemed easier to create *immediate desire,* and thus close the sale, with *tangible* products. The buyer can pay his money and take home his merchandise! Once the desire has been created for the tangible product, the buyer can have it *now.*

Although these three points may seem valid on the surface, the professional salesman with successful experience in selling intangibles knows that this is sheer nonsense! In fact, once he has *product knowledge,* he may perhaps *prefer* to sell *intangibles* over tangibles. *Why?* What advantages are involved? Let's find out more about intangibles!

Making "Intangibles" Become "Tangible"

Since there are many salesmen who believe that the tangible product is an "easier" sale, let us first demonstrate how the *intangible* product can be transformed into something *real* and *tangible.* Once it is established that we can make the intangible become tangible, then we will discuss the other advantages of intangible selling.

Let's take the example of Jim Wolfe who is a master at selling hospitalization insurance. Imagine the mental picture which he paints when he discusses the need for his product.

"Mr. Jones, with the high cost of medical and hospital expenses today, it is absolutely impossible for a person like yourself to consider carrying such a heavy financial burden and not have proper hospitalization insurance."

Mr. Jones smiles and asks, "Exactly what do you mean, Jim?"

With this, Jim pulls out a chart showing that the average hospital bed in his city for a private room has soared to $90.00 a day. He then continues: "Mr. Jones, what would you do if your wife, Susan, were to be told that she had developed a tumor on her lung and must undergo surgery at once? I just had a very dear client of mine, by the way, who experienced this horror—and through a series of operations, which kept his wife hospitalized for 145 days, they were able to save her life. It was only through her husband's hospitalization coverage, though, that he was able to sustain such a huge expense without being completely wiped out financially. Mr. Jones, you have worked a lifetime to accumulate a comfortable savings. Surely, you wouldn't want to have your lifetime's work completely wiped out, and even go into great debt, because you didn't have the foresight to plan ahead with proper hospital insurance."

Mr. Jones' hands begin to sweat as he pictures his wife lying in a hospital bed. The salesman has created a mental picture which has become quite *real* and *vivid!* What could be more "tangible" to Mr. Jones than this frightening scene painted so vividly in his mind? Buying hospitalization insurance no longer represents exchanging his money for just a piece of paper (the insurance policy). Instead, it represents a matter of *life* and *death* to his loved ones. Suddenly, the intangible has become tangible!

The successful mutual fund salesman also knows how to make his intangible product become tangible. As he tries to convince a client to purchase mutual funds with an investment of $100 per month, he hears the buyer reply, "What! $100 a month? Why, we can't possibly afford such an expense with all of the things we need for the house . . . a new color TV, living room furniture, a new refrigerator, and a complete paint job! Why, my car even has to be replaced soon."

It is obvious that this buyer can only visualize obtaining *physical products* with the steady monthly payment of $100 which was suggested. He can see no justifiable exchange when paying into a mutual fund that will return him nothing concrete for years!

The mutual fund salesman grins and says, "Look Tom, you are 45 years old and you haven't been able to save $1,000 in the past 20 years! If you don't change your present attitude, you're going to be an awfully sorry man someday when you have a real need for savings and nothing to show for it! Let's think about 20 years from now when you're 65 and no longer have the ability or energy or health to run your construction company. You have a *high* standard of living today—

and I think that when you're 65, you'll want the same high standard. You won't want to settle for Social Security!"

The salesman then pulls out a chart and shows his prospect the statistics which indicate the huge profits which his prospect could have made had he started investing in mutual funds 20 years ago. He then continues: "Tom, $100 per month would not have created such a heavy burden on you during the past 20 years. It wouldn't have taken food off your table, and it wouldn't have created a hardship on you and your family. Isn't that right?"

Tom nods, and the salesman continues: "Surely, $100 per month—or *more,* if you can afford it—won't change your standard of living today one iota. But it *will* make all the difference in the world at an age when you can no longer work. After all, what do you expect to do when you're 65? Give up your golf? Quit traveling? Drive an old car? Move to a cheap apartment? Or will you want to depend on support from your children?"

Tom now visualizes himself as an old man with plenty of spare time but with no money to do anything. He pictures himself having to ask his children for some extra spending money—such as he remembers his father doing when he had become old and penniless. What can be *more tangible* to Tom than the realization of such poverty?

The Chinese proverb, "A picture is worth a thousand words," certainly applies to intangible selling. Creating such a mental picture as we have illustrated

is definite proof that "you can make intangibles become tangible."

Appeal to Your Prospect's Imagination

The imagination of man has no boundaries.

Selling intangibles is the most creative form of
selling because it appeals directly to man's *imagination*.
A professional salesman can give his product unlim-
ited glamour; he can appeal to every emotion of his
prospect; he can paint a mental picture in his prospect's mind which can make every fibre of his being
tingle with an inner excitement unmatched by any tangible object!

A good example is the travel agent who creates a
"Garden of Eden" in his client's imagination as he
tells about the magic enchantment of a faraway South
Seas island vacation.

"There are only a handful of places left on earth
which offer such a complete escape from the hectic
world as we know it today." (At this point, the wife
comments about her husband's nerves and says, "He
just *has* to get away. It's business, business, business!
He never stops! He's a bundle of nerves!")

The imaginative travel agent recognizes a clue
and continues: "Just think. No telephones, no TV,
never putting on a dress shirt and tie for three weeks!
Picture yourself basking in the tropical sun with a cool
South Seas breeze spraying you with salt water from
the blue Pacific!"

As his clients half close their eyes, the salesman

notices the wife unbutton her heavy winter coat. She can actually *feel* the South Seas sun! Her imagination has no boundaries!

Napoleon said it: "The human race is governed by its imagination."

Selling intangibles is also governed by the salesman's imagination. Learn to develop your sales presentation so that you will appeal to your prospect's imagination . . . and you will always have him in the palm of your hand.

The Emotional Appeal

Certainly, most intangible products can have a powerful emotional appeal if a proper sales presentation is developed. This is obviously true with such products as insurance, securities, educational sales, employment agency services, and so on.

Howard Myers, a leading educational salesman for XYZ Business School, certainly knows how to appeal to his prospect when selling a business course to a high school graduate's parents.

"A high school education by itself means absolutely nothing today," he says. "What kind of a future do you want your son to have? The average high school graduate today will earn this amount in his lifetime (pointing to a chart)—as compared to the same man with a higher education." Howard's prospect may reply, "Why, I never realized that there could be such a vast difference!"

This is Howard's cue to press on: "Well, you must

understand that the future will be more and more an age of specialization. Your son's future will be a lifetime of struggling without an advanced education in a specific field."

This last point is the one that is apt to hit home. Howard's prospect will most likely ask something like this next: "Which course do you recommend that Thomas study?"

Once the emotional appeal has hit home, the intangible product has become quite *alive.*

A loved one's future is certainly a very serious matter, and his future happiness is a very *live* and *material* thing.

Intangible Products Are "Problem-Free"

For those readers who haven't already realized the many advantages of selling intangibles, here is a partial list:

1. There is not likely to be an *inventory* problem. You never have to worry about such things as color, sizes, etc.
2. Intangibles require very little storage space (if any) as compared to selling tangibles like automobiles, furniture, garden supplies, clothing, etc.
3. There are no shipping problems to be concerned with.
4. There are no production problems to be concerned with.
5. The outside salesman has no heavy cases to carry.
6. The outside salesman doesn't need a big car (or

station wagon) to carry samples.

7. Intangible products don't require a large area for display.
8. From a company standpoint, a lot of money isn't tied up in salesmen's samples.
9. There are no problems with styles or fads (such as being stuck with last season's miniskirts).

Generally, your overhead will be lower because there is no warehousing, no large showroom, no tax on inventory, no interest on financing an inventory, etc.

Conclusion

As illustrated, selling intangibles can be *a very easy and rewarding career.* Once you become good at developing your prospect's *mental picture* of your product, the intangible *"uncertainty"* ceases to be a problem. And, in light of the many advantages, perhaps you may want to further check the possibilities of selling intangibles in your area. Check around, and notice how well the professional intangible salesmen live!

XIX

PRACTICE, PRACTICE, PRACTICE... AND THEN PRACTICE SOME MORE

"Only salesmen and fisherman expect success without practice"*

Baseball superstar Ted Williams was once quoted in a magazine interview, as follows:

"They say the secret of my hitting is natural ability and good eyesight. A lot of people have as good eyesight as I have (20–15) and probably better, and still they're always ready to say eyesight's the reason he does it . . . and natural ability. That's so easy to say and to give credit for. They never talk about the practice. Practice! Practice! Practice! Dammit, you gotta practice!"†

*Clayton T. Knox, *Birth of a Salesman*, page 60; National Underwriters Company.
†"Subject: Ted Williams" (an interview with Jean Flynn Dreyspool), *Sports Illustrated*, August 1, 1955.

Williams went on to say that he never knew a player who practiced as much as he did. And the evidence, as gathered by baseball observers who followed this great hitter's career, would seem to bear him out. In fact, Williams was known not only to practice *before* a game, but also to practice *after* a game. Many times—and especially when he was dissatisfied with his performance in a particular game—Williams could be found (with possibly reluctant teammates and coaches) taking extra batting practice long after the crowd had left the ball park. This is why Williams could also say, with justification, that there had never been a hitter who hit more baseballs than he had. No wonder this man was a superstar!

Of course, Ted Williams is not the only great athlete who believes in practice. In fact, wherever you find a champion in the field of sports, you find a person who is dedicated to hard work—a person who spends many, many more hours than his teammates and opponents in practicing and thinking about his craft. Another outstanding example is Jack Nicklaus, who is considered by many people to be the greatest golfer in history. From the time he was a young boy in Columbus, Ohio, Jack Nicklaus wanted to be a champion golfer. His father, who shared this goal, taught Jack that the only way he could accomplish what he wanted was through constant practice. Thus, young Jack Nicklaus became practically a "fixture" around Columbus golf courses. Throughout his teens, he spent portions of nearly every day practicing golf. And even after becoming a PGA superstar, Nicklaus has continued to practice probably more than any other golfer. As a result, he (like Ted Williams in baseball) has undoubtedly hit more golf balls than any man in history. Therefore, it shouldn't be surprising that he's the leading money-winner in professional golf. Just think of that: The man who hits the most golf balls earns the most dollars!

Certainly, we could continue with many more dramatic examples from the world of sports—such people as Mark Spitz (swimming), Peggy Fleming (figure-skating), Frank Shorter (Olympic marathon), and others. But it isn't only in sports that practice "makes perfect." Consider, also, the crucial value of practice to the entertainer. Unquestionably, the ballet artist, the pianist, the operatic singer and the pantomimist must spend endless hours practicing and perfecting their arts and skills. So, too, must the comedian, the actor, the popular singer, and the thousands of "supporting" artists—the band musicians, the men and women in the chorus line, and all of the people who are true professionals in the entertainment business, whether of superstar status or not. (Unfortunately, the public often disapproves of the enormous earnings that some entertainers are able to enjoy . . . but if people would only stop and think about the countless hours, days and years of practice, preparation and rehearsal that the entertainer has endured, there would be less concern about the spectacular incomes that a few are able to achieve.)

Again, we could go on and on with examples of the importance of practice in many different fields and professions. The point is that practice is vitally necessary to *anyone* who wishes to excel in *whatever* he is doing. Of course, not all people are blessed with exactly the same amounts and same kinds of native or natural abilities. But, barring physical or mental handicaps, the differences among us are not so great that one man cannot equal the achievements of another through hard work, dedication and practice. In most cases, practice will be the equalizer.

The sales field is definitely no exception to this rule. As a professional salesman, you must fully appreciate the power of practice. Oddly—and unfortunately—many salesmen do *not* understand this. Many believe that "instinct" is more important—that you can't improve on the fine points of selling by study or practice. Sure, it's easy to see why the athlete, the ballerina or the violinist has to practice and develop his or her techniques. But too many salesmen seem to believe that the great performers in their profession are "born, not made." Too many put their trust solely in what they like to call "natural sales ability." While it may be true that there is such a thing as a "salesman's personality," it is also true that the outstanding salesman does not rely on this trait alone. He improves upon nature. He studies to find out what he can do better, to sharpen his techniques, and to learn new or different approaches from the experiences of other salesmen. And then he *practices* what he has learned! He practices religiously . . . over and over again . . . *before* and *after* his actual sales presentations.

How Does a Salesman Practice?

All right. Let's assume now that you are convinced of the *value* of practice. The next question is
how do you do it?

In all fairness to those many, many salesmen who
do not regularly practice at their profession, it must be
said that they simply don't know how to get started. It
seems so much easier, for example, for a ballplayer to
practice. There are so many concrete, definite things
he can do to make himself stronger, faster, quicker
. . . or to help him hit the ball better, or catch it or
throw it. In other words, practicing in athletics seems
to be more clear-cut; and the results can be more
easily and quickly measured. At least, that's the way it
seems. But, in any event, we should not be concerned
about what is harder or easier. We should be concerned about the *results* of practicing in *your* profession. Those results, of course, are measured in terms
of sales made, and sales lost—and, ultimately, in terms
of dollars earned.

So, how do you get started? Well, for one thing,
you might ask yourself when the last time was that you
practiced your sales *presentation. Not* the last time you
gave the presentation to an actual prospect—but the
last time you *practiced* it. Have you worked on it at
home recently? Or in your office . . . privately? Have
you recorded it on tape and played it back and listened
to it . . . once, twice, three times, a dozen times? Have
you stood in front of a mirror and given the presenta-

tion to your own image? Have you enlisted your wife to play the role of a prospect and listen to your presentation? In other words, have you *rehearsed* your presentation—and then *analyzed* it? If you haven't, then it's high time you did! You'll be surprised how much you can learn about yourself. How you *sound.* How you *look.* Whether you're the kind of man you'd want to do business with yourself! You can study your posture, the way you walk and the way you stand, the way you use your hands, how you hold your head, and whether your eyes look down or straight ahead at the man you're addressing. You can get the feel of your own voice—whether it has the ring of confidence, enthusiasm, friendliness. And you can look for possibly annoying habits, such as twitches, finger-tapping, shifting from one foot to the other, jingling coins in your pocket, or overworking certain words or phrases. In short, you can put yourself on stage, exposed to the toughest audience in the world—*yourself* (and your wife, whenever she's participating).

Another thing you can practice is your *introduction*—or your first meeting with a new prospect. Again, you can use all or most of the same techniques that we've just discussed. You can stand in front of a mirror, rehearse with your wife, or record your voice on tape. You might also practice actually walking into your new prospect's office, or walking up to him in the lobby of a hotel or a restaurant. You can even carry your brief case during such dry runs. At any rate, don't overlook the importance of the way you handle yourself during an introduction. This part of your repertoire as a salesman deserves every bit as much practice as any other.

A third area where practice is vitally important is in the *demonstration* or *description* of your product. This is especially true when the product or service is highly technical, or sophisticated or unusual. But it is also important for the less complicated and less sophisticated products. Whether you sell computers, industrial machinery, insurance . . . or vacuum cleaners, housewares, or fishing tackle . . . you must not only *know* your product but also be able to *communicate* its features to your customers. A potential buyer will have little confidence in what you wish to sell him if you, yourself, don't appear to know how it works or how to use it—or if you can't demonstrate its use to him. You might, in fact, be unusually knowledgeable about what you're selling—but can you impart this knowledge to your prospect? Can you smoothly, efficiently and convincingly *show* what your product or service will do for him? In other words, are you a good demonstrator? Ask yourself this question. Chances are, you won't be *entirely* satisfied with the answer. If you're honest with yourself, you'll probably have to admit that you need to re-examine your demonstration techniques. But don't be discouraged, because you're not alone. Every salesman needs to be constantly on guard to see that he doesn't let his demonstrations become too routine, too automatic, too clumsy. Sometimes there's even a tendency to lose sight of, or to gloss over, some of your product's best features. This might happen after you've made a few "easy" sales and have become over-confident. But there's one tremendously effective way of preventing this kind of slippage or sloppiness in your demonstrations. And that is *practice!* Just as you practice to achieve and maintain poise in your introduction and style in your presentation, so also should you practice to achieve and maintain accuracy, dexterity and completeness in your demonstration.

The fourth major selling skill that demands continuous practice is the *close.* Almost every salesman—amateur or professional—will contend that the close is the toughest part of selling. It's the "moment of truth." It's the point where a prospect becomes a customer, where a contract is signed, or where the money changes hands. But, for all its importance, how often do you suspect that the working salesman actually practices this part of his repertoire? The answer is: Not very often! Too many salesmen rely on their instincts, on their ability to "fence" with the prospect—instead of on a carefully developed and practiced closing technique. But you can be sure that the *top* salesmen, the men who make the *big* money and enjoy the highly successful careers, do *not* neglect this vital phase of their business. They *do* practice. They *do* think about how they will close their sales. They go over it in their minds and they often rehearse it out loud—to themselves, to their wives, or to their associates. They develop—and *practice*—their timing, pacing and rhythm. And it is this kind of concentration, dedication and determination that separates them from the "average" salesman.

Conclusion

Practice is so important in the field of selling that some of the leading sales organizations in our country have invested significant amounts of money in instant-replay, audio-visual systems to help their salesmen practice. Of course, these systems are nice to have. They improve upon—and speed up—the process of practicing. But, essentially, they do the same job as you, yourself, can do by looking into the mirror, rehearsing with your wife or an associate, or using an inexpensive tape recorder. The point is that you *must practice*—with whatever means you have at your disposal. Some men may have what appear to be greater "natural" or "inborn" selling traits; but you *can* match them if you are willing to work at it—if you are willing to *practice*.

To start yourself thinking in the right direction, you might consider the words of a couple of great performers in other fields.

Somerset Maugham, giving advice to young authors, said:

> ". . . to write well does not come by instinct; it is an art that demands arduous study."

And Calvin Coolidge had this to say:

> "Nothing will take the place of persistence; talent will not; nothing is more common than unsuc-

cessful men with talent. Genius will not; unre-
warded genius is almost a proverb. Education will
not; the world is full of educated derelicts. Persistence and determination are omnipotent. The
slogan "Press On" has solved and always will
solve the problems of the human race."

XX

KEEPING PHYSICALLY FIT

Although physical fitness by itself would not appear to have much to do with salesmanship, we believe that we would be negligent if we didn't direct some attention to the subject. Physical fitness is "a way of life"—and it definitely should be incorporated into the daily life of the professional salesman.

Self-Discipline

Without question, self-discipline is an important trait to anyone—in any profession. It is, in fact, just as important to the businessman as it is to the athlete. And it's every bit as important to the salesman. There are many times in the salesman's life when self-discipline is crucial. There are times, for example, when he must *force* himself to work, whether he feels "up to it" or not.

The professional salesman should have a regular

212

program of physical development and personal care aimed at maintaining his health and vitality. Regardless of how late he went to bed the previous night, and no matter how many drinks he may have consumed, he should religiously carry out an exercise program the following morning. Sometimes it may mean doing it with a hangover—but regardless—he should do it! It is this kind of discipline which becomes a part of his life—and that makes him a top producer in selling.

Physical Fitness Means Extra Mileage

Without question, keeping physically fit will give a salesman much needed extra mileage during his daily work. The expression, "a good body makes for a sharp mind" is not just idle chatter, but is a medically proven fact.

Notice how vibrant a trim, well-conditioned businessman appears—and notice how keen and quick his mind is.

Obviously, keeping physically fit, by itself, will not *add* to a person's intelligence; but it *will* make a difference in alertness, vitality and mental responsiveness.

The salesman who is physically fit will not tire during the middle of the day, as do many physically weaker salesmen. Having that extra stamina towards the end of the day is a tremendous edge. This is especially true for the salesman who makes evening calls, such as the life insurance agent, the mutual fund salesman, the educational salesman, and so on. Although their prospects may be exhausted at the end of their days' work, the "night" salesmen who function with vim and vigor will have a definite advantage over the unconditioned salesmen who are ready to collapse, right along with their customers, in the middle of their evening calls. *Physical fitness gives you extra mileage that will mean extra sales.*

The salesman who is in poor condition will literally not be able to make those extra calls at the end of a long day. Think of the sales that he will lose because of his lack of energy! He certainly cannot work at the same pace as the salesman who keeps in top physical shape.

The next time you go shopping in a department store that stays open until 9:30 P.M., notice how the overweight salesmen are "dragging" at the end of the day. Notice how their lack of energy causes them to lean on the counter, or even sit in a comfortable chair towards closing time. In the final hours of the long working day it is the energetic, physically fit salesman who gets the orders from the last-minute shoppers who must buy before closing time!

Conclusion

Physical fitness is a *way of life.* It requires a great amount of self-discipline and must be pursued on a daily, *routine* basis, whether you like it or not. A career in selling requires the same discipline. Begin a physical fitness program immediately . . . not only will you get additional sales, but also, as a fringe benefit, you will feel better and probably live a longer, more enjoyable life.

XXI

THE SALESMAN'S COMPENSATION

Just a few brief thoughts on the subject of compensation for the salesman. It is the opinion of the authors that you can't publish a book on salesmanship without some discussion of how a salesman should be paid. After all, we don't work for our health!

Without question, the salesman who works on a straight commission basis is the highest paid of all salesmen. Granted, there is a certain amount of risk involved—but if you are *good,* there is no other way to earn as much money. The commissioned salesman gets paid what he is *worth.* If he produces, he is well paid; if he does *not* produce, he still gets paid what he is "worth."

Working on a straight commission basis is the closest thing to being self-employed as you can come to without actually being a proprietor of a business. As it is with almost all facets of our free economy, the greatest profits are normally generated from those ventures which offer the highest risk. A salesman who works on a straight commission basis is *gambling* that he will produce more than what an employer would normally be willing to pay him for similar work. At the same time, he is gambling that he can generate more commissions, which will exceed a salaried sales job, even though he is not guaranteed any income whatsoever if he does not produce. He is confident of his ability to be better-than-average. He forsakes a steady income of "X" number of dollars every week because he realizes that his annual earnings will average out to be higher than the fifty-two weekly paychecks which are paid regardless of production. All the commissioned salesman has to do is learn to *budget* his commission checks—since sometimes he may face feast or famine. In the long run, however, the man who produces is always financially ahead.

A quick review of the salesmen who generate the highest incomes will reveal that if you want to earn *big* money, you must be willing to work on a commission basis. If you are good, and you are willing to work hard, you'll be way ahead of the game.

The Salaried Salesman

Many salesmen would prefer to have their cake and eat it too. They don't want to risk gambling on being paid solely by commission, so they take a sales position which pays them by salary. They, and their wives, know that regardless of how many sales are made there will be a guaranteed paycheck every payday. Sure, it's nice to be able to budget according to a fixed amount of income each and every week—and perhaps even get a small bonus at the end of the year! But, if you are really worth your salt, do you realize how much this kind of "security" *costs* you every year? If you are a top producer, you will not need the security of the salary. Instead, you'll be paid more commissions than what an employer would be willing to pay in advance on a guaranteed basis. If you're *not* good, then realistically speaking, how long do you think your employer will be willing to pay your salary? It is the opinion of the authors of this book that *somebody* always gets short-changed when they sell on a salaried basis. The employee either gets paid too little in proportion to what he sells, or the employer pays the salesman too much for the small amount of volume he generates. In either case, there are likely to be repercussions eventually. If you are not selling enough to meet your salary, it is obvious that it is just a matter of time before you will be looking for another sales job. Therefore, as long as you are producing enough to warrant a salary, wouldn't you prefer to be paid what you are worth?

The Fringe Benefits

Never take a job because it offers good *fringe* benefits. If you think that the position is exactly what you want, then take the fringe benefits as icing on the cake. Only if all other things are exactly equal in two seemingly identical jobs, should your decision be based on the fringe benefits which the jobs offer.

Actually, fringe benefits are methods by which you are paid *in lieu of other compensation*. Thus, whatever the value of the fringe benefits, you can literally add the costs of such benefits to your annual income to determine what they are actually worth. Don't forget, however, to take into consideration that group life and health insurance are paid for you and you don't have to pay taxes on their costs when paid by an employer (within certain limitations). Thus, if you are selling furniture at the rate of 5 percent straight commission, and your sales volume is $1 million per year, you will gross $50,000 annually. Don't think that it's a good deal when the company offers you extra fringe benefits —company car allowance, expense account, insurance, and so on—when at the same time, your commission will be lwoered to 3½ percent! Don't think that this "new deal" is in your best interests unless you can calculate that: (1) the costs of these new fringe benefits exceeds the 1½ percent cut in commissions in an actual dollar amount ($15,000), and (2) your sales volume will be lower in the future.

Of course, there are other fringe benefits such as pensions, stock options, paid vacations, use of the company summer home or yacht, and so on. And these, too, must be properly evaluated to determine their real value. We are not suggesting that a company offers fringe benefits solely to "take advantage" of the salesman. We are only suggesting that you recognize what these fringe benefits *may cost you in lieu of other compensation.* Quite often, a company will pay fringe benefits because it genuinely cares about its people. In these cases, you can consider the fringe benefits to be "something extra"—or just a good deal!

Is There a Happy Medium?

There are all sorts of combinations between a salaried sales position and a straight commission sales position. For the person who does not have a sufficient amount of savings (or staying power) these are the ideal happy mediums. Many companies offer a base salary *plus* commission. Naturally, the commission will be a lower percentage because the salary will be paid in lieu of "X" amount of commissions otherwise paid. To the novice salesman, this is a very satisfactory arrangement. Also, there are companies who guarantee a weekly "draw" which is applied against future commissions. When it is guaranteed, it is noteworthy to determine in advance whether you are, in fact, borrowing money which must be paid back or whether the company is actually "guaranteeing" that you will earn a fixed amount of income each pay period.

Many companies will pay a weekly or monthly draw against commissions, which simply means that they will advance their salesmen commissions in a fixed amount so that his family can rely on a steady income for family budgeting purposes. For example, a salesman who represents "Short Pants Manufacturing Company" can sell "Bill's Clothiers, Inc.," in January, but the goods won't be shipped until May, and the terms will be 90 days after shipment. Instead of the salesman waiting six to eight months to be paid, "Short Pants" advances him commissions based on his production. This method of paying a draw against commissions is mandatory for many salesmen so that they can survive until they receive the payment of their commissions after the goods are delivered and paid for. Other companies advance commissions to the salesman based on the orders placed, even though the goods have not been received by the customer. Obviously, most salesmen prefer a system that gives them a draw against commission, regardless of their weekly production in any given period of time, because they want to avoid the "feast or famine" situation which accompanies the straight commission sales position. Of course, the seasoned pro has enough of a balance in his savings account that he does not need this financial assistance. Not all salesmen, however, have built up a such a cushion.

Conclusion

Without question, the commission salesman has the opportunity to earn the greatest income—that is, with all other factors being equal. The top five percent of all salesmen in the United States are working on a commission basis. And undoubtedly, the *big producers* whose annual incomes are in six figures and up are all being compensated for their talents *by commission*. No company pays salaries in these ranges to their sales force. Remember: If you want to be paid *exactly what you are worth*, work for a company that pays a fair commission based solely upon your *efforts* and *results*. The professional salesman will rarely consider any other basis for being paid.

XXII

TOTAL COMMITMENT

"Total Commitment: Without it you're, at best, average. With it, you *excel.*"

... *Robert L. Shook*

If you want to be the *complete professional salesman* as illustrated in this book, it will take some doing on your part. As with any profession, there is a great deal of knowledge to be obtained. It will take much toil and effort. You will have to work hard in order to develop the selling techniques which this book presents. And, once you have absorbed the wealth of knowledge contained in this book, you'll still need one more thing to make it work. In order to achieve the desired results, you will have to give a TOTAL COMMITMENT.

It is the authors' opinion that the key trait shared by all outstandingly successful people is a sense of

TOTAL COMMITMENT. Thus, in order to be THE COMPLETE PROFESSIONAL SALESMAN, you, too, must make a TOTAL COMMITMENT.

Look around you. Study the highly successful people whom you know. If you were to look for one common denominator in the character of these people, you would discover that they all have a Total Commitment that they apply to their work. This is the key trait shared by all "big achievers"—whether they be in industry, the sciences, the arts, entertainment, sports, or SELLING. Without it, at best, you will have to settle for mediocrity. But *with* it, there is no limit to what you can achieve.

A Total Commitment is a way of life which anyone can adopt and practice. It is a winning quality which is available to everyone. Once you have made your Total Commitment, you will possess a new strength— and a new power that comes from within you. It will pervade your life and will drive you to do what's necessary in order to become the *complete professional salesman.* All of the knowledge which you have learned in this book will then become an intrinsic part of your experience and your consciousness., Each morning you will wake up with a strong desire to *sell.* Nothing will discourage you; you will refuse to accept defeat. You will treat every momentary failure as part of the price which must be paid to gain success. Whereas the failures are the part of selling that conquer most salesmen, *you* will *not* fail. Whatever you choose to call it —"determination" . . . "guts" . . . "will power"—all of these fine human qualities come from having a TOTAL COMMITMENT.

Total Commitment is a special ingredient which all eminent people possess. Study the lives of the great people of the past . . . they all had it. Certainly, George Washington, Benjamin Franklin, and Thomas Jefferson had a Total Commitment. Winston Churchill, Marie Curie, and Ben Gurian had it. How about Thomas Edison, Alexander Graham Bell, and the Wright Brothers? And don't forget people like Glenn Miller, Cole Porter, and F. Scott Fitzgerald. These are great individuals whom the history books tell us had a Total Commitment.

But please remember: Total Commitment is not a thing of the past. It still exists—and it *always will.* Jack Nicklaus, Pete Rose, and Mark Spitz are fine examples of athletes today who display a Total Commitment. Barbara Streisand, Bob Hope, Patricia Neal—they've got it, too. Barry Goldwater, Bill Lear, W. Clement Stone, Howard Cosell, Leonard Woodstock, Neil Armstrong . . . all of these people represent just a few of our great *living* Americans who have a Total Commitment. Successful people in all fields have this wonderful quality. And the *top salesmen* with all companies also have it! You, too, can be an outstanding individual, because *you* also can have a Total Commitment.

Think, for a moment, about what TOTAL COMMITMENT can mean to you in any number of circumstances in your life. For example, if you had been totally committed, you might have been a high honor student in high school or college. Or perhaps when you tried out for the football team or the debate team, a Total Commitment would have made a very big difference. And, how many jobs have you had where you didn't get the results you wanted because you lacked that special drive—that special quality—TOTAL COMMITMENT?

On a larger scale, what would the results have been in Viet Nam if a Total Commitment had been given by the United States? And what about our war against cancer and the war on poverty?

Yes, a Total Commitment can make a tremendous difference in just about every facet of our lives, both private and public.

Study other salesmen you know. How many salesmen have you seen who have excellent education, long and outstanding work experience, fine speaking ability, a very pleasing appearance, and everything else it takes to be successful . . . and yet, they fail? On the other hand, you can study highly successful salesmen who do not, on the surface, appear to have as much going for them—but who are nonetheless *big producers.*

Perhaps now you can see how a Total Commitment can make a big difference.

A leading sales organization recently made a study at its convention where its top salesmen were being honored for their fine production records. The owners of the company wanted to study these men to find out what common denominator they shared. Top management reasoned that, if such a common denominator did, indeed, exist, an understanding of it would prove invaluable in selecting and developing future salesmen. The study showed that these men were not "gifted" with the stereotyped qualities so commonly associated with salesmen—qualities such as dynamic personalities, extreme extroversion, bubbly enthusiasm, and so on. Instead, after extensive interviews, it was discovered that the one common denominator which existed among the entire group was *Total Commitment.* Each man possessed a positive mental attitude and excellent working habits. Their common denominator was something which *every* salesman can possess. It's entirely up to the individual!

Don't just scratch your head and wonder how other salesmen in your field—salesmen who seemingly have less ability than you—are able to do such a big job. Perhaps they are totally committed . . . and *you aren't.* This won't be the first time that this was the case. If ever there was a "success secret" in life, *this is it!*

Think it over. A Total Commitment in selling can make a big difference to you. It's something which is available to all salesmen. Why don't you make sure that *you* possess this winning quality . . . ?

XXIII

CONCLUSION: THE COMPLETE PROFESSIONAL SALESMAN

Now that you have decided to make selling a career, you have two choices: (1) Either approach it as a *profession* . . . put forth a full effort . . . learn your job thoroughly . . . study your product . . . organize . . . *live it!*—or (2) think of it as "just another job" . . . resign yourself to the non-productive life which results from mediocrity.

This is *your life!* And the time has come for you to take inventory of it and decide exactly what you want to make of it. Do you want success? Or you are willing to settle for mediocrity? Remember: The price of success is high . . . but compared to the drabness of being ordinary, the payout is immeasurable.

The Professional Approach

Every salesman should approach his career as a *professional*—and as a professional, he will want to become completely engrossed with the goal of becoming an expert in his work. He will strive for perfection; he won't settle for less! He will want to master every facet of his daily work. Just as the professional golfer exerts his energies to perfect his driving or putting, so too will the professional salesman strive to become a master of his trade. Just as the doctor studies into the late hours of the night to understand newly discovered medical achievements, so too will the professional salesman keep abreast of changes in his field. And just as the scientist searches for new worlds to conquer, so also will the professional salesman accept new challenges as they arise. Through sincere dedication to his profession, the salesman will raise himself head and shoulders above the crowd.

The professional salesman will not be satisfied with his skill until he feels that he has completely perfected it. He will *practice* and *practice* each phase of selling until he achieves super-excellence. He will spend many of his days off and weekends in practice sessions. Sure, this will be a sacrifice, but he knows it's worth it. He will stay up late doing research and keeping abreast of the changes in industry and the latest advancements of his competition. He will study all the information available concerning his products, his industry and his competitors. He will search for new ideas that can be applied to his profession. He knows that if he works, studies, has enthusiasm and sincerity, and has a positive mental attitude, he will succeed. He cannot fail. He will combine theory, experience, positive thinking and effort—which equal success.

Only when the professional salesman has a complete understanding and working knowledge of the sophisticated selling techniques illustrated in this book will he have the self-confidence to really *know* that he is a top professional in his field. Only with this inner belief in himself will he have that very special kind of confidence which we refer to as *sales confidence*.

The thing that *you*— as a professional salesman— should be most concerned about is whether *you* have *Sales Confidence*. It's the key to your success! *If you make a total commitment, you can become the complete professional salesman.*

About the Authors . . .

Who are Herb and Bob Shook? And why are they qualified to write this book, THE COMPLETE PROFESSIONAL SALESMAN?

Herb and Bob Shook are a father-son team. They are, perhaps, the finest father-son selling combination in the country.

Herb Shook, born in 1912, lives in Pittsburgh, Pennsylvania. He is president of American Executive Corporation, a holding company; president of Shook Associates Corporation, a national sales organization; and president of American Executive Life Insurance Company. He is a dynamic speaker and has lectured to national corporations throughout the country on the subject of sales incentive programs. He is a graduate of Duquesne University.

Bob Shook, born in 1938, lives in Columbus,

Ohio. He is Chairman of American Executive Corporation, Shook Associates Corporation, and American Executive Life Insurance Company. He is a graduate of Ohio State University.

The success stories of these two energetic men are quite interesting and inspiring. In September, 1961, they formed a partnership called Shook Associates. This organization sold health and accident insurance to business and professional people.

The partnership had a very humble beginning. An office was set up in the basement of Herb Shook's home, and the father and son began calling on business and professional people in the community. Once they developed an effective sales presentation, they decided to recruit other agents to sell their product. They reasoned that they could teach other men how to present their product to the public in the same manner in which they were selling.

Soon, the Pittsburgh area was enjoying much prosperity, and Bob (who was then 25) moved to Columbus, Ohio, to open what was to be the first of many out-of-state sales agencies.

The rest is now history. Other agencies were opened, and one of the nation's great sales organizations took shape. Today, Shook Associates Corporation (SAC) has a network of salesmen in major marketing areas throughout the United States.

As the business grew, the Shooks decided that their sales volume warranted owning their own insurance company. Thus, in January, 1973, the American Executive Life Insurance Company was born.

Next, a holding company—American Executive Corporation—was established. This firm now owned SAC and American Executive Life Insurance Company.

Beneficial Standard Life Insurance Company of Los Angeles, and Fidelity Interstate Life Insurance Company of Philadelphia, are the underwriters of all business written by the Shooks' marketing organization; and American Executive Life Insurance Company reinsures 50 percent of the business which is sold by SAC.

Just *what* did the Shooks do to develop a marketing organization large enough to warrant the formation of their own insurance company?

Remember: It took only twelve years to build such an organization from scratch—and today SAC sells more new premiums than the majority of the insurance companies in America. That's quite an accomplishment in such a short period of time. And according to the Shooks, they have just begun to expand!

"During the next decade," says Herb Shook, "we will make our early years look like we were standing still!"

The answer to the question of "What did they do" to accomplish this is right here in their book. They dedicated themselves to becoming a *professional* sales organization—and they practiced the selling methods and principles outlined on these pages.

As outlined in THE COMPLETE PROFESSIONAL SALESMAN, SAC goes "by the book." First, an effective sales presentation has been developed

—and this presentation is learned *verbatim* by all salesmen.

"If it sounded canned," says Bob, "we would throw it out. It wouldn't be worth the paper it's written on!"

The Shooks believe that if there is only one "best" way to present their product, *every new man* should learn his "best" way before he develops any bad habits.

Second, a complete training program is followed to the letter by all sales managers. Each new man is *field-trained*. And, although this one-to-one basis for training new men is quite time-consuming, it is nonetheless very effective. All sales managers also are fully educated in how to properly field-train a new man. The new man is given considerable homework for the evenings and week-ends when he is not in the field.

Third, sales seminars are conducted weekly to continually motivate the sales force. Sales management offers top financial opportunities with SAC, and promotion follows only if a man has a good sales record in the field. Thus, men are highly motivated because there are advancement opportunities.

By offering a truly outstanding sales position with high earning potential and an opportunity for sales management, SAC has been able to attract top quality men. Throughout the industry, SAC has established a reputation for its ability to recruit the highest caliber men ever developed by a single agency in large numbers. The typical SAC salesman, for example, has five years of college education and a strong selling or business background. On the average, he has also been earning $15,000 a year prior to joining SAC. Herb and Bob Shook have found that this "average" SAC salesman will generate *three times* the amount of new sales produced by the "average" salesman in the insurance industry as a whole!

Every salesman is thoroughly trained in complete product knowledge, and is expert at handling objections which prospects may throw at him.

But at SAC, the salesman learns much more than product knowledge. He is also taught *how to sell.* He is taught how to prospect, how to organize his time, how to approach a potential customer, and how to close a sale. In short, the SAC salesman is trained and educated to be a *professional.*

Communication: The SAC Secret of Controlling a Large Sales Force

Bob Shook believes that communication is the secret to running a large sales organization.

"The telephone," says Bob, "is the best bargain in America for a company who has out-of-town salesmen."

Each SAC salesman reports three times per week to his immediate supervisor. During these telephone conversations, they discuss problems, successes, and opportunities.

"There's nobody more lonely than the out-of-town salesman," according to Herb Shook. "He doesn't see other co-workers for long periods of time and he has no one to talk with about his good days or bad days."

At SAC, however, each man is as close as the nearest telephone. Collect calls are always encouraged —and in fact, the Shooks *insist* that if a salesman doesn't make regular collect calls to the home office, then SAC management will call the salesman *collect.*

Sales seminars are also conducted on a regular weekly basis in all sales territories. These seminars are not of a "pep-talk" nature. Instead, they are *educational* —and they deal with various selling techniques and principles. The Shooks believe, in fact, that their salesmen don't need pep-talks or special "motivational" help. On the contrary, the SAC salesman is a professional who knows how to motivate himself and build his own incentive.

Herb and Bob also strive to keep communications lines open by making personal visits to the field and hosting regular meetings and special events. Both men visit every branch office at least twice a year. They also hold an annual Executive Management Meeting —usually lasting four days—and always held in an interesting location. (One such meeting, for example, was held in conjunction with a Caribbean cruise.)

A Family-oriented Organization

Since SAC originated as a small family business, it was only natural that the same kind of close-knit "family" atmosphere be perpetrated as the organization grew. For example, there are no "employees" with SAC—only *Associates*. The personal problems of the salesman become the problems of the Shooks. Every man in SAC knows that he can call collect to Herb or Bob at any time . . . at the office or at home. The wives of the salesmen are also included in all social events—and every such event is geared toward making the wives a part of the organization. In fact, wives are even encouraged to attend sales seminars.

"The salesman's wife," says Bob, "is a sexy sales manager who sees the salesman every day of the week. It's vital for her husband to have her support. She must share in his enthusiasm."

The Father-Son Relationship

Without question, one of the strongest things that Herb Shook and Bob Shook have going for them is their close working relationship.

Perhaps every father dreams of someday working in business with his son; yet, as we all know, very few ever realize this dream. Partnerships often encounter difficult problems, even where the partners are not related—and when you add the emotional element of a family relationship, the partnership often encounters unbearable strain.

But the Shooks have successfully bypassed this pitfall. They have a beautiful and very effective working relationship—one that engenders admiration and respect from the people around them. "Perhaps my being headquartered in Columbus, Ohio, and my father being based in Pittsburgh is a bigger factor than we realize," says Bob. "If the two of us were constantly under the same roof every day of the week, perhaps we would get in each other's way like other fathers and sons who work together."

Whatever the reason, the Shooks are a winning father-son combination whose love and respect for one another is a delight to all.

Both as a team and as individuals, Bob and Herb bring a number of potent personal qualities to bear on their business lives. And in spite of their father-son relationship, they both strive hard to be highly objective and constructively critical where SAC and its success are involved.

It isn't only an admiring son speaking, for example, when Bob says:

"Herb Shook, in my opinion, is the best salesman in America. When I tell people he sells nine out of every ten prospects, I get looks of disbelief. But it's true . . . and, in fact, I find it hard to understand why the tenth prospect doesn't buy once Herb has made the presentation.

"Frankly, I doubt if there is *anybody* who can motivate a group of salesmen in a seminar the way he can. He has the enthusiasm and drive of a 'super-ego'—yet he's sincere and humble.

"Sometimes I think he's almost too much of a 'positive thinker' . . . especially when he sets our annual sales goals . . . but darned if we don't always manage to reach those goals. That has to tell you something about him and his selling philosophy!"

Likewise, it isn't just a proud father speaking when Herb analyzes Bob's selling success:

"He's successful," explains Herb, "partly because he's the most self-confident person I've ever known. But more importantly, he has excellent work habits and he keeps himself highly organized—which allows him to accomplish twice as much as men with equal ability but less purpose.

"One of the best ways to describe him is as 'a man who won't quit'—a highly competitive man who insists on winning.

"All in all, I don't know of any man his age in the country who has learned as much as he has about selling and about developing an effective sales organization."

In summary, Herb and Bob Shook have all the necessary credentials to talk knowledgeably about successful selling. They've *been there*. Their record speaks for itself. Each one of them is a COMPLETE PROFESSIONAL SALESMAN.

More importantly, they've studied the reasons behind their success, and they've collected those reasons and put them into a down-to-earth, understandable story which can benefit thousands of other salesmen.

Vast opportunities exist within America's Free Enterprise System—opportunities for any salesman who is willing to put in the right amount of effort aimed in the right direction.

There's plenty of room . . . in fact, there's a *need* . . . for professional salesmen in America. Through this book, *you* are invited to help meet that need. You are invited to become **THE COMPLETE PROFESSIONAL SALESMAN.**

Ronald L. Bingaman